The Art of Defending
Part One

1v1 through 8v8

Wayne Harrison

REEDSWAIN

**Library of Congress
Cataloging - in - Publication Data**

by Wayne Harrison
    The Art of Defending
      Part One - 1v1 through 8v8

ISBN No. 1-59164-032-6
Lib. of Congress Catalog No. 2002094147
© 2002

Editing
Bryan R. Beaver

Printed by
DATA REPRODUCTIONS
Auburn, Michigan

Reedswain Publishing
612 Pughtown Road
Spring City, PA 19475
800.331.5191
www.reedswain.com
info@reedswain.com

BOOK ONE
THE ART OF DEFENDING
1 v 1 THROUGH 8 v 8
(INCLUDING SMALL SIDED GAMES AND FUNCTIONAL PLAYS)

CHAPTER FOUR
DEFENDING IN A 4 v 4 SMALL - SIDED GAME

CHAPTER FIVE
DEFENDING IN A 6 v 6 SMALL SIDED GAME

CHAPTER SEVEN
TEAM SHAPE AND MOVEMENT IN AN 8 v 8 SMALL SIDED GAME

CHAPTER EIGHT
FUNCTIONAL WORK THROUGHOUT THE UNITS

CONCLUSION AND DISCUSSION

CHAPTER ONE

INTRODUCTION TO DEFENDING

This book is part one in a two book series on the art of defending, it covers defending in 1 v 1 situations through to defending in 8 v 8 small sided game situations but includes functional situations also.

The companion book covers defending in "Phase Plays" and builds up to 11 v 11 full game situations and it is the natural progression from this book.

Between the two books, aspects of defending are discussed and evaluated in great detail.

I hope you enjoy this book and it encourages you to delve into the realms of defending in phase plays and 11 v 11 game situations in Book Two.

Defending is an overlooked part of the game and time is often not spent on the art of defensive play as opposed to the art of attacking play. It could be related to the fun factor. Everyone likes to score goals and shoot at goal in training and games but defending doesn't have the same glamorous appeal.

Nevertheless, defending is an integral part of the game of soccer; after all, we can't enjoy the feeling of attacking and scoring goals if we don't learn how to defend properly as we need to win the ball first before we can build an attack to threaten the opponent's goal.

The art of good defending in practice and in game situations takes a disciplined mind and body and all players should be taught how to do it properly.

Defending begins with the first player closest to the ball when it is in the opponent's possession and this can mean a striker being the first line of defense trying to win the ball back in the attacking third of the field. Strikers in particular have to be educated to understand that they too have an important role to play in defending; too many think their job is done when they are successful only with the ball. Not true!!!!! The closer to the opponent's goal your team can win the ball, the better chance there is to score a goal, so strikers must understand they need to work hard to regain possession of the ball for the team.

The first myth the coach has to conquer therefore is that defending is only important for defenders. This is not the case. All players in the team have a responsibility to learn how to refine this art and become good at it to the benefit of each individual and to the team as a whole.

This book begins with basics of 1 v 1 defending, the most prevalent part of defending in the game. Soccer is a game of many 1 v 1 situations all over the field and the individuals who are proficient at this skill will give their team a greater chance of winning the game so it is very important we start at the basics.

As we go through the book we build up the numbers of players involved to develop the theme, increasing the numbers in overload situations both to our advantage and against us to provide real tests of the players' abilities in defending.

Each situation, be it 1 v 1 or 3 v 3 is broken down into the key coaching points to make the explanations clear and concise.

As we progress through the chapters in the book the theme changes from purely technical defending skills to tactical defending skills. The change is gradual and consists of different percentages of the combinations of technical and tactical defending. When we get up to the 8 v 8 situation and defending as a team, the emphasis is strongly focused on the tactical side of defending, though there is still work needed within the framework of the team to include technical defending also.

Defending through the thirds becomes an important aspect of defending as we get into the 6 v 6 and 8 v 8 game situations.

I like to promote the practice of defending through the thirds from the front third or attacking third, and work back through the team, through the midfield third, and back to the defensive third, working on each unit in turn, then bringing the whole team together and working collectively to defend well and win back the ball. This starts with the technical side of defending and as we develop the theme the tactical side becomes more prevalent as the numbers of players involved increases.

Defending then becomes a co-operative process between teammates trying to win the ball back for the team.

I hope this book helps you the coach help your player to become at least proficient and at most consistent and ultimately effective in the art of defending and that the players get joy from their successes. Their reward for consistent, efficient, worthy defending (regaining possession of the ball), will be ultimately the team scoring a goal and those who won the ball to provide this opportunity should celebrate their part in the process also.

If you want to take your education into the 11 a side game, try the second book in the Art of Defending series. You will then cover your needs from a defending perspective all the way through from the most basic 1 v 1 defending to the more complicated 11 v 11 situation.

In this book we are always defending working with the numbered players only. The lettered players are always the attacking opponents to be defended against.

Defending principles can be categorized into a logical process for the coach to follow and implement in training. They can be broken down into the following key coaching points:

PRESSURE
SUPPORT
COVER / BALANCE
RECOVER
TRACK
DOUBLE TEAM
REGAINING POSSESSION & COMPACTNESS

What does this all mean?

PRESSURE

This is when the individual defender closes down a player on the ball to exert pressure on him to give the ball up. It can result in the player on the ball being pressured into making a bad pass, mis-controlling it, or the defender being able to tackle the player and dispossess him by either kicking the ball away or challenging and winning possession. These instances all result in possession being lost by the attacking team due to the pressure exerted by the first defender.

Pressure does not always result in a change of possession immediately, so the defender can jockey the attacker to stop his forward momentum and give time to teammates to get into position to help win the ball back.

SUPPORT

This is the position taken up by the second defender to act as help for the first defender. The first defender, by his stance, can show / force the attacker towards the support player (second defender).We will talk later about angles and distances of support and communication with the pressuring player. These are the three essentials that are needed for the support player to be effective.

COVER / BALANCE

This refers to the positions of the next line of players away from the first two defenders, particularly the third defender who is next closest to the pressure and support players. This player provides a balance (1st, 2nd, and 3rd defender) behind the pressure and support players. Beyond this third defender you can work with the next closest players and integrate their positioning into your coaching session.

RECOVER

Players in position on the field in front of where the ball is being defended must make it a priority to run back and position behind the ball, if possible between their own goal and the ball that is in the attacking team's possession. They recover back (recovery runs) to help the team by getting more people between the ball and their own goal to make it more difficult for the attacking team to score. They must recover back along the shortest route so they get back as quickly as possible but into a position where they are most effective in terms of the positions of the ball and the opponents.

TRACK

The attacking team's players will make forward runs into dangerous positions on the field and this is where defending players need to follow or track their runs to mark them and prevent them from getting free and able to affect the game. Tracking runs can be short or long depending on the distance of the opponent's runs.

DOUBLE TEAM

It is possible to help the pressing player win back possession of the ball by closing down the space (pressuring) around the attacking player on the ball from another angle, preferably from the other side to where the first pressuring player is positioned. This is almost closing the player on the ball down from his blind side and can be very effective in regaining possession of the ball due to the fact that the attacker doesn't see the second defender coming so can't take immediate action to avoid having the ball taken off his. In some circumstances triple teaming can occur where three players all close the player on the ball down simultaneously and this can prove very effective in regaining possession of the ball.

REGAINING POSSESSION AND COMPACTNESS

Here the defending team has won back the ball and are now the attacking team and look to play it forward as soon as possible.
As the play is developed up the field it is important the team push up the field to add continued support to the player on the ball, but also to affect the positions of the opponents and take them away from their goal should possession be lost again. The whole team moves forward and this will result in the compactness of the players from the back to the front of the team.

COACHING METHODOLOGY

To be effective a coach should be able to change to different coaching methods to suit the moment. We all have our own style; some do it quietly, some are more demonstrative, and some are more vocal (but don't commentate). As long as it is done in a positive manner and creates positive results, all styles can be effective.
Coaching Style is based on personality, temperament, our philosophies on how the game should be played and on the ages and abilities of the players we are working with. There is no one universal style, every coach is different.
Coaching Method is different, the methods you use to coach are important in getting the best out of your players and you should be able to base your coaching around three different methods which can be implemented in various degrees at different times.

COMMAND, QUESTION AND ANSWER AND GUIDED DISCOVERY

1. COMMAND METHOD

The coach decides, the players listen and comply but do they really listen, do they learn or most importantly DO THEY UNDERSTAND?
Using this method the coach can't be sure if the players understand what they are doing or why they are doing it, or if they are simply following directions.
Were you right in what you told them?

For example you tell a player to move to a certain position on the field and he does it. Does he know why he needs to be there? Maybe, but you cannot be certain. In a game situation will he know where to go?

2. QUESTION AND ANSWER METHOD

The coach tries to stimulate the player into a response to a direct singular question. For example, "Where should you pass the ball in that situation?". The player needs to think for himself and you know immediately if he understands or not by his response.

3. GUIDED DISCOVERY METHOD

The coach leads the players to make their own decisions. For example: "Show me where you should go to help the player on the ball". Again the players have to think for themselves and are more likely to remember and learn from their self determined action.

Soccer is a game of the moment and players, not coaches need to decide at that moment what they should do on the field and we need to help them to make that decision for themselves. What we have is a Command Method (autocratic / bossy) and a Co-Operative Method (democratic / guiding) but sometimes also a good coaching approach may involve saying nothing, letting them play / practice with no direction. Just watch them. This is more important than some realize.

WHY CO-OPERATIVE?

1. It helps players become thinkers and make their own decisions.
2. Fosters relations between coach and player by sharing the decision making process.
3. Players enjoy it more.
4. As well as having skills, players develop the ability to chang situations, exhibit discipline and maintain concentration.

HOW DOES IT HELP THE COACH?

The coach needs more skill and knowledge. Because players can have several solutions to one problem, they are seldom absolutely right or wrong, but you as the coach need to have an answer. This improves you as a coach as you yourself need to think more deeply about your solutions to problems. External factors can influence the method used. For example, a large group of unfamiliar players need more of the Command Method where a smaller familiar group of players need more of a Co-Operative Method of coaching.

CONCLUSION

Based on the above discussion it is clear that soccer is a game of free flowing play and the players need to be developed to be the decision makers much of the time. The coach needs to help them get there by encouraging them in training to work it out for themselves and, when they can't, guide them to the right decision. Game situations are difficult because you often don't have time to ask "where should you be now?" but over a period of time and with patience the players will take on more responsibility on and off the field and improve their performance because of it. A by- product of this which must not be overlooked is that the coach himself will improve his ability and knowledge as a consequence of using this approach.

HOW TO ORGANIZE A SESSION PLAN

1. ORGANIZE THE EQUIPMENT (BIBS, BALLS AND CONES)
2. COACH ONLY ONE TEAM AT A TIME TO AVOID CONFUSION
3. COACH (AFFECT THE ATTITUDE OF) EACH INDIVIDUAL PLAYER IN THAT TEAM
4. STAY ON THE SAME THEME
5. USE DESIGNATED START POSITIONS TO BEGIN EACH PRACTICE TO PAINT THE PICTURE YOU WANT TO CREATE
6. LIST THE KEY COACHING POINTS
7. THINK INDIVIDUAL / UNIT / TEAM – SIMPLE TO COMPLEX AND DEVELOP LOGICAL PROGRESSIONS INTO THE SESSION
8. SPECIFY THE SIZE OF AREA USED AND MAKE IT RELEVANT TO THE NUMBERS AND ABILITY OF PLAYERS USED
9. DIVIDE THE FIELD INTO THIRDS FOR EASIER POINTS OF REFERENCE IN SMALL - SIDED GAMES
10. USE TARGET GOALS, TARGET PLAYERS, OR LINES FOR OPPONENTS TO PLAY TO IN PHASE PLAYS AND FUNCTIONS
11. ISOLATE THE AREAS AND PLAYERS IN FUNCTIONAL PRACTICES TO KEEP IT SPECIFIC
12. USE OFFSIDE WHERE NECESSARY FOR REALISM
13. COACHING METHOD: FREEZE THE COACHING MOMENT (STOP, STAND STILL), REVIEW WHAT WENT WRONG, RE-RUN SLOWLY (CAN BE WALKING PACE), RE-CREATE THE SET UP AND GO AT MATCH SPEED. LET THEM PLAY
14. USE A QUESTIONING / GUIDING COACHING METHOD RATHER THAN COMMAND
15. FOR ATTACKING THEMES LIMIT THE NUMBER OF TOUCHES THE OPPONENTS HAVE IF THEY WIN THE BALL

16.   FOR DEFENDING THEMES LIMIT THE NUMBER
           OF TOUCHES THE DEFENDING TEAM HAS
           WHEN THEY WIN THE BALL.THIS ENSURES
           THE OPPONENTS HAVE THE BALL FOR THE
           DEFENDERS TO TRY TO WIN BACK

CHAPTER TWO

DEFENDING IN 1 v 1, 2 v 1, 2 v 2 , 1 v 2, 2 v 3 AND INTRODUCING 3 v 3 SITUATIONS

INTRODUCTORY SESSION WITH NO OPPOSITION THEN PASSIVE OPPOSITION

20 x 20

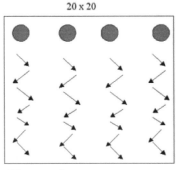

Diagram 1

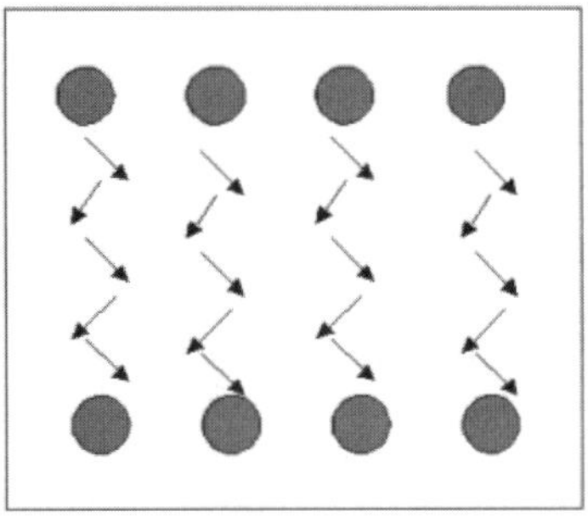

Diagram 2

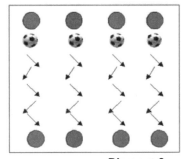

Diagram 3

Diagrams 1 , 2 and 3

a)   Players are sideways on running backwards to the other line, changing sides in defensive mode. Increase pace.

b)   Shadow heading and running back on coach's command.

c)   In two's, one running moving side to side, the other running backwards, changing to a sideways on stance checking opponents run.

d)   Ball between two working as above, working back and forward, defender shadowing the ball not winning possession.

e)   Practice feinting to tackle with your front foot, forcing attacker to protect the ball.

HOW TO DEFEND EFFECTIVELY IN 1 v 1 SITUATIONS

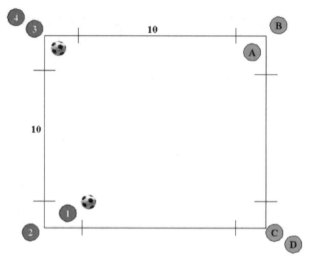

Diagram 4

1.   Player (1) passes the ball into player (A) and follows the pass to close the space down and defend against (A) and try to regain possession of the ball.

2.   Once these two have participated in their 1 v 1 and taken it to its conclusion, then it is the turn of defending player (3) to pass the ball into attacking player (C) to work in the diagonally opposite way across the grid.

3.   You can set the session up with the players working up and down the grid instead of diagonally across it if you prefer.

Session Plan

a)   Receiver (A) tries to score through defender (1)'s goal.

b)   Work both sides and alternate numbered players and lettered players.

c)   All players get the chance to attack or defend.

d)   Encourage and praise good defending.

e)   Correct the faults.

f)   Step in and demonstrate to **show** the players what is needed if required, demonstration is better than explanation.

g)   When the defender (1) wins the ball set a target for this player to score a goal as a reward for winning the ball.

h)   Once the players have practiced these techniques a while you can make it competitive by counting the number of goals scored by each player on each team. This is a way of measuring the success rates of the defending players winning possession of the ball individually and as a team. It can help by providing feedback to the players as to how successful they are at winning back the ball and defending successfully.

i)   The same process can be used in all the small sided games taking the winning of the ball alone initially as the reward, to making it competitive by winning the ball then trying to score from the gained possession and to have a positive reinforcement from it. For example, in the 2 v 2 or 3 v 3 games count the goals scored by each team from regained possessions and the first to 5 goals is the winner. Rotate each team receiving the ball to attack.

DEFENDING IN a 1 v 1 SITUATION

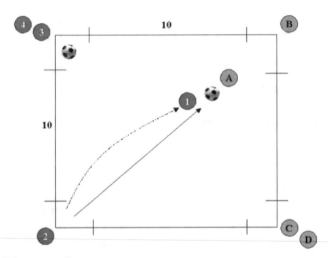

Diagram 5

COACHING POINTS OF INDIVIDUAL DEFENDING – CLOSING DOWN

1.   **Travel as fast** as possible as the ball travels to close down opponent.

2.   **Close** the opponent down with a curved run, forcing the player the way you want him to go (if you have time to do so).

3.   **Slow down** the last few yards, get balanced, bend knees, sideways on stance forcing the play your way, and slow the attacker up (making play predictable).

4.   **Feint to tackle** – use your front foot; this forces the opponent to protect the ball and ultimately look down at the ball and away from you (also prevents awareness of where support players are in a game situation).Try to steal with front foot.

5.   **Watch the ball,** not the player so you aren't thrown by body movement.

6.   **Stay on your** feet and be patient, your chance will come to win the ball. If you go to ground you give the initiative to the attacker.

7.   Think about the way you want to player to go, it can be onto your opponent's weakest foot or to the side you are strongest and most confident. It can depend on which side there is less space for the attacker to work in to restrict his movement and options and to make play predictable.

8.   Encourage the players to not only win the ball but also to maintain possession if they can. In this session they can win it and try to score into the other goal as a reward for gaining possession. In this instance both players will get a chance to practice defending in the same sequence.

1 v 1 PREVENTING AN OPPONENT FROM TURNING

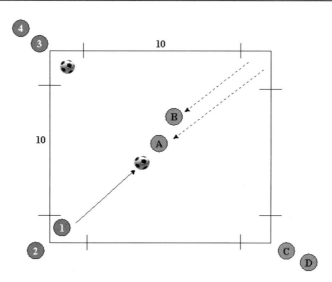

Diagram 6

1.   (1) Passes to (A), (B) closes down and stops (A) from turning and scoring. Previous coaching points but also get touch tight to attacker. You can judge the distance by actually touching the back of the player.

2.   Move with the player to maintain the same distance between you. If the attacking player goes back away from your goal, keep the same spacing by moving with him, not allowing him to turn and face you by increasing the distance between you.

3.   If you are too far away the attacker can and will turn and face up to you, creating a 1 v 1 situation which is a great advantage to the attacker. Too close and the attacker can spin off you, using the feel of your body as momentum to spin away quickly into space behind.

4.   The time to tackle is when the attacking player is half turned and consequently not protecting the ball with his body. Until then be patient and wait for the moment to strike. If you force the attacker to pass the ball back you have done your job effectively, but if it results in you either taking the ball off him by kicking it away or better still winning the ball and maintaining possession you can then turn defense into attack.

DEFENDING WITH a 2 v 1 ADVANTAGE: PRESSURE AND SUPPORT

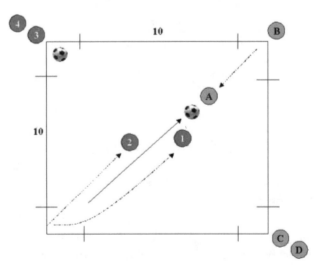

Diagram 7

Session Plan

1.   (1) passes to (A) and closes down quickly with (2) in a support position.

2.   (1) Closes down (A) with a curved run, forcing the attacker to have to play towards the supporting player (2), thus creating a 2 v 1 situation in favor of the defenders.

3.   The two defenders should be able to create a situation where they can win and also maintain possession of the ball.

4.   Coaching points include:

    a) Support Angle: 45 degrees to the pressuring player.

    b) Support Distance: close enough to be able to affect the ball if the pressuring player is beaten.

    c) Communication: the supporting player can advise the pressuring player where to force the attacking player to go. A simple command is best such as right or left or right shoulder, left shoulder so the pressuring player knows where the support is.

    d) The run of the pressuring player (body language) may dictate to the supporting player where to go also. If the pressuring player makes a curved run to show the attacker to the left then the supporting player will take up a position to support on that side. They must react off each other. There isn't always time for the supporting player to tell the pressuring player which side to show the attacker so this is a two–way communication situation: the pressuring player using body language and the support player using speech to communicate.

In terms of the distance of support, a factor to consider is the type of player you are up against; is the player quick, is the player a good dribbler? If the player is quick and the pressing player and the supporting player are close then the ball can be kicked past both of them in one movement to beat them. If the player is a good dribbler and the two defenders are far apart then the player can beat the first defender and have room to work to beat the second defender also. Therefore the correct distance between the two defenders is vital for them to be successful: not too close and not too far apart. 3 to 5 yards would be about right to cover both instances.

DEFENDING IN a 2 v 2 SITUATION: PRESSURE AND SUPPORT

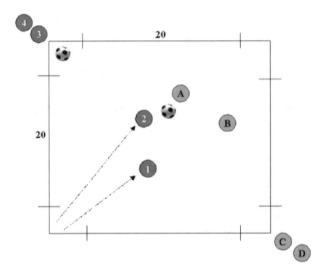

Diagram 8

Develop:

1.   2 v 2 with (B) joining in. In a 2 v 2 show the "piston effect" of support movements as the ball travels. Also consider that the closest player can close down the ball as it travels from player to player (discussed later).

2.   (2) closes (A) down and shows **inside** to the support player. (1) Supports at a 45 degree angle but is also screening (B). In the 2 v 1 situation (1) only had to think about supporting (2) but now there are two things to consider:

supporting (2) and screening the position and movement of (B).

3.   Distance of support depends on the position on field and the speed and ability of the opponent. The support player can give verbal direction but also can take a position with regard to where the attacker is forced as previously discussed. It can depend on which happens first, the body position of the pressing player forcing the play one way or the verbal direction of the support player advising forcing the attacker towards his position.

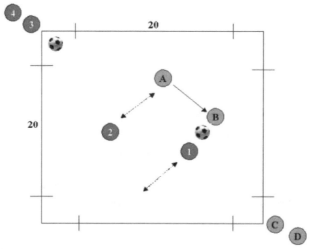

Diagram 9

4.   (A) Is on the ball, (2) pressures and (1) supports, at the same time shadowing (B).

5.   (A) passes to (B), (1) and (2) adjust their positions as shown, now (1) pressures and (2) drops back into a support position, but at the same time shadowing (A).

6.   (2) can also close down (B) if closer than (1) as an alternative.

7.   (B) passes back to (A) and overlaps, adjustment can be as above i.e. (1) marks (A), (2) shadows (B)'s run so defenders don't have to cross over.

DEFENDING IN A 2 v 2 SITUATION: MARKING ZONES

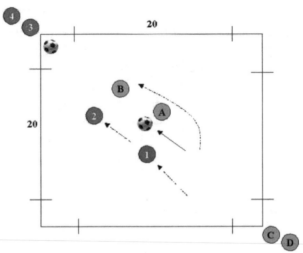

Diagram 10

1.   (B) Passes to (A) and overlaps. Defenders can do the following: (2) can take the overlapping player (B) while (1) takes (A). This means they switch the marking.

2.   The alternative is (1) tracks across to follow (B) on the overlap so they still mark the same players.

3.   See thefollowing page to see the result of this second move where we are dealing with man marking as opposed to marking zones as above.

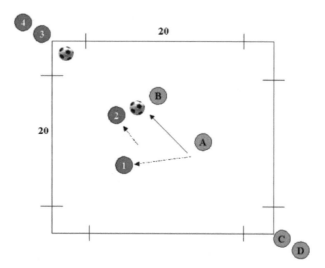

Diagram 11

1. This action needs very good communication between players and constitutes marking zones as opposed to marking players.

2. Players need to communicate quickly and efficiently to effect this movement successfully.

3. The ball has been passed from (A) to (B) and (2) has left a position marking (A) to a position marking (B).

4. (1) Takes the shortest route and drops into a support position for (2) who shows the player (B) inside.

DEFENDING IN A 2 v 2 SITUATION: MAN MARKING

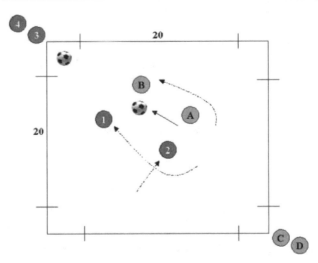

Diagram 12

1. This second course of action is easier for the players to understand as it constitutes man marking so they just follow the same player.

2. It means more work for (1) who must cover a greater distance to track the run of (B) but if players don't communicate well or quickly enough this is the correct course of action to take.

3. (2) would now drop back into a support position to help (1) and (1) would be best advised to show (B) inside now towards the support of (2), thus preventing (A) and (B) from getting behind them.

DOUBLE TEAMING IN a 2 v 2 SITUATION

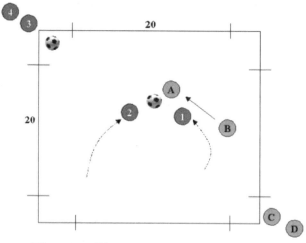

Diagram 13

1. Instead of using a "piston" type of movement which constitutes (1) closing down (B) on the ball and (2) supporting with the correct angle and distance but also taking up a position to be ready to mark (A) if the ball is passed as in the previous diagram, there is an alternative method of defending (see above).

2. Here the ball is passed from (B) to (A). If (1) is closer to (A) then he closes the ball down in a way that prevents (A) from being able to pass back to (B); this is called getting in the passing lane. (1) may need to close down in a curved run to (A).

3. This creates a 2 v 1 situation in favor of the defenders as (1) forces (A) towards (2). This is called **double teaming** the player on the ball cutting out (B).

4. The only danger is that the defenders must make sure they do not leave a space between (1) and (2) where (A) can pass the ball to (B) who has moved into the space in front.

5. Pressuring from two players **quickly** from two angles should be enough to win back the ball and prevent this.

6.   This is a more **aggressive** type of action and is designed to win back the ball quickly and efficiently. The piston type of defending in two's is a more patient, delaying type of action.

DELAYING IN A 1 v 2 WITH A RECOVERING SUPPORT PLAYER

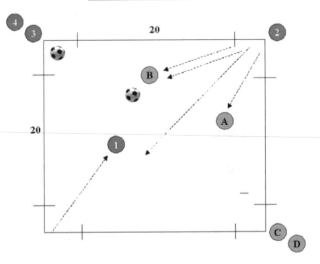

Diagram 14

1.   (1) must **delay** the forward motion of the two attackers until (2) can join in. You can condition it to 5 seconds before (2) can join in to help.

2.   (1) takes up a position between the player on the ball, the attacking support player and the middle of the goal to keep the defensive balance. The purpose is to delay (A) and (B); hold them up until (2) can get into a position to support and create a 2 v 2.

3.   (2) makes a recovery run along the shortest route (along a line to the center of the goal) to get into a support position for (1).

4.   Alternatively (2) can double up on (B) and attack the ball

from the opposite side. The diagram above shows both recovery runs that (2) can make.

5. As (2) is getting into a support position for (1), this is the signal for (1) to put full pressure on (B).Previous to this (1) was in a delaying position between the two players encouraging them to pass the ball to each other but keeping it in front. (2) can also offer information as he recovers; "you press the ball" for example.

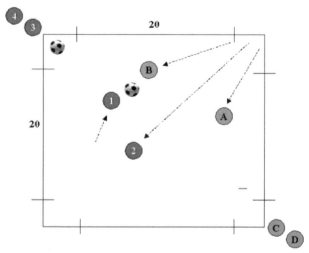

Diagram 15

1. Here we see where (2) has recovered back to support (1) and as (2) gets into position, (1) closes down (B) forcing the player inside to the support.

2. (2) now has the job of supporting (1) involving the coaching points of angle, distance and communication, but also to shadow the movement of (A).

3. (1) has done a good job of delaying the forward motion of (A) and (B) to enable (2) to recover back.

4. The recovery run is best along a short route, but must not be too short or too long. Too short and the support for (1) will be too flat and the ball can be played in behind (2) for (B) to run onto in space; too long or deep and there will

be too much space for (B) to receive the ball. (2) has to be close enough to close down (B) as the ball travels and arrive in a good pressuring position as the ball arrives at the feet of (B).Better still, can (2) intercept the pass as it travels from (A) to(B)? The timing of the interception has to be exact here.

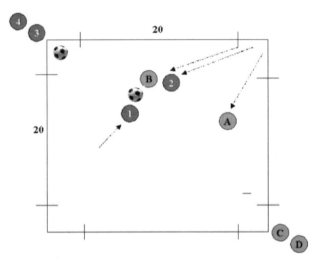

Diagram 16

1. Here we show how the recovering player can double up on (B) to help (1) win the ball.

2. The timing of this movement has to be good because if (1) closes too early, the space is open for an easy pass from (B) to (A) and the defensive movement doesn't succeed.

3. There is always the chance of the ball being passed between (1) and (2).

4. To stop this (1) can close down and show (B) outside, away from (A) and step into that passing lane to (A) creating a 2 v 1 in favor of the defending team.

5. These are options for the recovering player to consider, it will depend on the moment in the game as to what he should do.

THE ART OF DEFENDING: THE GUIDING TRIANGLE

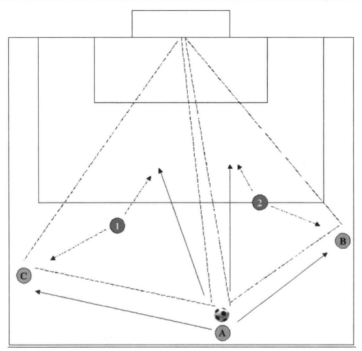

Diagram 17

1.   If the ball is played from (A) to behind (1) or (2) the defenders should be first to the ball. If it's played to feet the defenders have time to close the attacker down as the ball travels.

2.   The Triangle takes its' shape from the player on the ball, the center of the goal and the player each defender is marking. The defender should position inside the triangle. The closer to the ball the closer the defender marks the player, the further away from the ball the more the defender marks space.

3.   From the defensive position the defender can see both the ball and the immediate opponent.

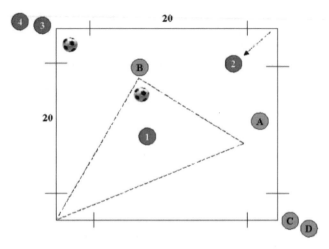

Diagram 18

1.   (1) takes up a position inside the guiding triangle. The guiding triangle is determined by the position of the ball, the supporting player and the goal. Here a balanced position between the ball, the support player and the center of the goal has been achieved by (1).

2.   (1) must constantly adjust position to accommodate the movement of the player on the ball and the support player with the view of keeping the ball in front.

3.   To help the defender, because there is no keeper in the goal, the attackers have to run the ball into the goal. If it were just a case of passing it into an empty goal it would be almost impossible for the defender to stop. The reality is that in a game the defender, if caught in a 2 v 1 against, would at least have the keeper in goal to help.

4.   (1) positions slightly towards the side to invite a pass from (B) to (A) to help delay their forward movement. As the ball is played across, if (1) can't intercept the pass then at least the ball has been kept in front. The secret is not to get too close to either player as this invites a pass in behind. (1) must maintain depth to avoid this.

5.   If (1) was confident enough and a good enough defender then a 1 v 1 situation could be created by closing quickly and showing (B) outside using body position to block off a pass to (A) and at the same time trying to win the ball. This would be the least likely course of action to take if there is the chance of delaying and getting help.

GETTING INTO THE WRONG POSITION

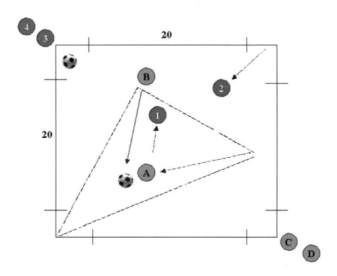

Diagram 19

1.   (1) gets too close and too flat with regard to attacker (B)'s position and invites a ball in behind for attacker (A) to run onto and score unopposed.

2.   Taking up this position (too close to one player) means his progress is not delayed and (2) does not have time to recover back to help (1) prevent a goal.

3.   (2) is on the way back with a recovery run but has no time to complete the run and get into a helpful defensive position.

ANOTHER FORMAT FOR 1 v 1's, 2 v 1's AND 2 v 2's

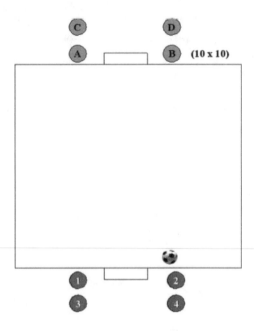

Diagram 20

1. If you want to set your session up in a different way to get the same results, this is an alternative idea. All coaching sessions for 1 v 1, 2 v 1, and 2 v 2 can be set up this way, the only difference being that the players work up and down the field, not diagonally across it.

2. Using this straight forward set up may be less confusing for less experienced coaches.

3. Develop 1 v 1's, 2 v 1's, 2 v 2's etc, with the size of area increasing as the numbers increase. It can range from 10 yards square up to 20 yards square with any distance in between depending on the ages of the players.

EXAMPLE OF A 2 v 2 SESSION

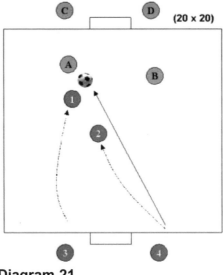

Diagram 21

1.   (2) Passes to (A) and both (1) and (2) close (A) down. (B) supports (A) in a 2 v 2.

2.   All previous coaching points are relevant and need not be repeated here as this is just serving as an example of a two v two in this format.

3.   Use whichever set up you are comfortable with; straight up and down the playing area or diagonally across the playing area.

A 2 v 3 WITH A RECOVERING DEFENDER

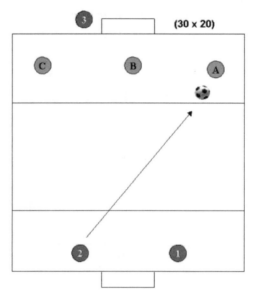

(30 x 20)

Diagram 22

1.   A bigger area to play in, we now have a 30 x 20 area with two goals to play to. You can include keepers if you like to make it more realistic.

2.   (2) passes to an attacking player, in this instance (A), and both defenders need to close the ball and players down quickly but in a position to delay the forward movement of the attackers until their team mate (3) recovers back behind the ball to help them. Have a time limit. For example, (3) counts to five before recovering so the attackers know they have to break quickly to score.

3.   This then becomes a 3 v 3.

4.   You can introduce the condition that the attackers have to cross a certain line to score if there are no keepers. Or leave it open so the pressing player has to defend well to stop a free shot at goal.

INTRODUCTION TO 3 v 3 DEFENDING

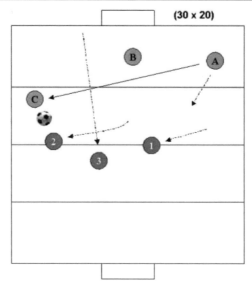

(30 x 20)

Diagram 23

1. (A) passes the ball across the field to (C) and (2) adjusts position across to press the ball.

2. (3) recovers back along the shortest route back to goal and gets into a good support position to help (2). The recovering player offers information to the pressing player as to where they will recover to.

3. (3), the original pressing player, now drops back into a covering position to help (2) and (1) and will adjust position according to the movement of (A).

4. All three defending players here are in a very comfortable shape to defend the ball and try to regain possession.

5. As the ball was passed from (A) to (C), (3) may have opted to close down (C) from behind if (2) hadn't moved across to pressure.

6. (3)'s recovery run into a supporting position must not be so deep that the support position can't help the pressing player (2).

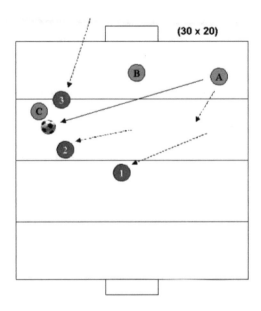

Diagram 24

1.   Here the recovering defender goes to the ball as this player is the closest to the ball and this is the shortest route back to affect the play.

2.   (2) moves across to press the ball and (1) moves across to get into a support position leaving (A) alone but with an open stance to still be aware of (A)'s position.

3.   If the ball is transferred back across to (A) then (1) is close enough to move back across and become the pressing player.

4.   If (3) gets back quickly enough to press the ball then (2) can get into a support position and still shadow (B) and (1) can drop into a covering position and still shadow (A).

CHAPTER THREE

DEFENDING IN a 3 v 3 SMALL - SIDED GAME

ESTABLISHING THE ESSENTIAL KEY COACHING POINTS IN DEFENDING USING THE 3 v 3 S.S.G. MODEL

DEFENDING IN a 3 v 3 + KEEPERS SITUATION

In this sequence the session includes using the offside rule from the compactness diagram. If movement of players takes defenders into unrealistic positions in relation to the real game through not using the offside rule, then introduce offside earlier, even from the beginning of the 3 v 3 sequence if necessary. You, the coach, have to judge this for yourself depending on the age and experience of your players.

Make the game competitive once the defending principles have been established so there is a measure of success in regaining the possession of the ball.
For example, count the number of goals scored from a regained possession but restrict the number of touches or passes to 5 before scoring a goal, because it is defending we are working on primarily, not attacking play.

In the following examples, if the numbered team wins back possession of the ball using the defending principles worked upon they have 5 passes to score a goal. If they don't do so within those passes the game restarts to ensure we work on defending again as the principle.

Ultimately let the game go free and just have a small sided game.

BASIC SET UP AND KEY COACHING POINTS

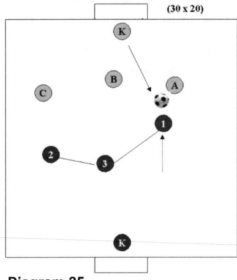

Diagram 25

1.   Player nearest the ball pressurizes the ball with team-
      mates in support and covering positions depending on
      the positions of the opposition and the ball.

Dealing here with first, second and third defender scenario, look-
ing at pressure, support and cover / balance positions of the
defending team.

Coaching Points:

a) Mark space (zone play) then **pressing** the ball, (1)
     closes down (A) quickly.
b) Making play **predictable** - show the player on the ball
     inside or outside depending on where the **support** is.
     If outside, then (1) has to be confident of winning the
     ball because this can result in a 1 v 1 situation.
c) Shape of the team (**covering / balancing** positions).
d) **Recovering** and **Tracking** - getting back behind the
     ball either into space or tracking a run from an oppo-
     nent.
e) Double Teaming.
f) Compactness.

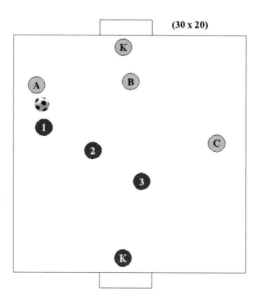

(30 x 20)

Diagram 26

1. Here the attacking team has tried to spread out the defending team and create bigger spacing between them. This can be highly effective and is what the team in possession should attempt to do.

2. The defending team has worked to the first three defending principles of pressure (1), support (2) and cover / balance (3) and tries to stay as close together as possible to fill the immediate spaces around them while being in a position to close down their immediate opponents.

3. Notice (3) takes up a deeper position for any ball played in behind or long in a covering position for (1) and (2) while also being responsible for (C) should the ball go to him.

PRESSURE

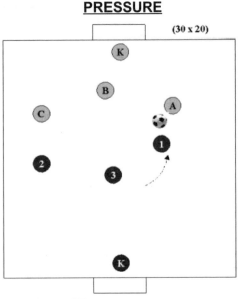

Diagram 27

1.   Working with the pressuring player. (1) tries to close down at an angle, forcing (A) into the support player (3) inside.

2.   (1)'s job is to make play predictable for (2) and (3) to help them position properly. By showing (A) inside, these support players know what (1)'s intention is and where they can be of the most help in supporting and covering.

3.   Forcing (A) into the numbers, although it is towards the goal, is the correct decision in this instance, as that is where the strength of the team lies.

4.   The defenders are strong here with depth so no ball can be played behind them and each attacking player is shadowed.

5.   At the same time they are positioned close enough to be able to travel as the ball travels to close down their immediate opponents should the ball be passed to them.

SUPPORT

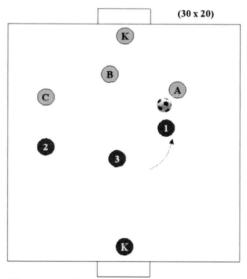

Diagram 28

1. The support player (3) positions in such a way that should the ball be passed to (B) there is time to close down and.

2. The key points here are angle, distance and communication; angle about 45 degrees, distance about 3 to 5 yards, and all the time offering advice to (1) with commands such as "show left", "left shoulder", or just say "left". Keep the commands short and too the point to help the pressing player know where to show or force the player.

3. It could happen that (1) shows the player outside and prevents a pass inside to (B) or (C) by positioning between them and the ball and here (3) could move outside also to create a 2 v 1 in the defender's favor.

COVER / BALANCE

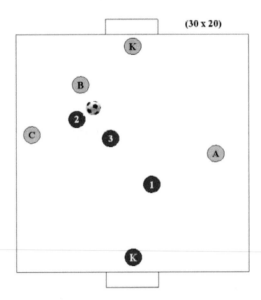

Diagram 29

1.   (2) shows (B) inside to support player (3).

2.   Cover / balance player (1) has to provide defensive depth for (2) and (3) but also take up a position in relation to where (A) is positioned.

3.   Should the ball be played through to (C), then although (3) should deal with him, cover player (1) is in position also to make a move to cover (C).

4.   The players' covering position in this example is a fine balancing act as there are so many variables due to the positioning of the opponents.

ADJUSTMENT OF PLAYERS

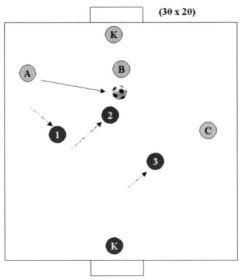

Diagram 30

1. The ball is passed to (B) in the center of the field and the supporting player from the previous set up (2) now becomes the pressuring player.

2. (1) drops back from a pressuring position into a supporting position for (2) and is also guarding the space if a ball is played in behind for (A) to run onto.

3. (3) is still the covering / balancing player but because the ball has moved closer to (C), he must position closer also while at the same time maintaining depth for all the players.

4. (3) gets into a position where if the ball is played to (C) then he is close enough to travel as the ball travels, to arrive in a pressuring position as the ball arrives. If (3) can anticipate the move quickly enough then an interception of the pass may be possible. Worst case scenario must be that (C) doesn't get too much time and space on the ball to get a good run at (3) in a 1 v 1 situation.

RECOVERY RUNS

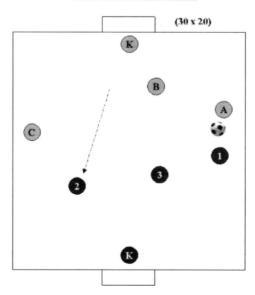

Diagram 31

1.   The lettered team have attacked forward and got themselves into a strong attacking position, creating a 3 v 2 in their favor.

2.   (2) has been caught too far forward (possibly from a previous attack where they have just lost possession of the ball) but recognizes the situation and makes a recovery run back behind the ball. Where this run is made depends on the position of (C) (his immediate opponent) and the position of teammates (1) and (3).

3.   (2) Is now covering both (3) and (1) but also in a position to close down (C) should be ball be switched.

4.   This is an example of an effective recovery run to help teammates and to be in a position to mark an opponent should he receive the ball.

5.   If (C) were to make a run forward it would force (2) to track (shadow) that run. Likewise if (B) makes a run forward then (3) is required to track that player's run.

DOUBLE TEAMING

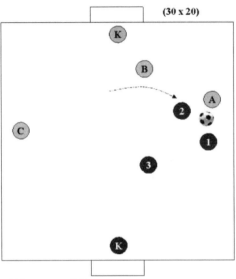

Diagram 32

1.   (1) closes down and pressures (A), (3) gets into a support position to help (1), assuming the correct angle and distance and offering advice, while (2) uses the chance created by these two holding up (A) to close down quickly and double up on the player on the ball.

2.   This movement must be quick and efficient; when we double up on someone it usually means we have left someone else free on the field. In this case (C) has been left free. If (A) manages to get a pass to (C) before the doubling up can be effective then (3) will adjust across the field to apply pressure.

3.   (2) must also try to close down (A) along the line of the passing lane to (B) to prevent a pass back and an escape for the attacking team. But often it is just a case of closing as quickly as possible because there isn't time to do this and regain possession of the ball.

TRACKING PLAYERS

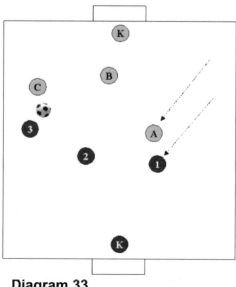

Diagram 33

1. (A) make's a forward run into a dangerous area of the field to threaten the defending team. (1) is the closest player and must track this run to prevent (A) from getting free.

2. (1) must make sure to stay goal-side of (A) and have a couple of yards in advance on the attacking player.

COMPACTNESS

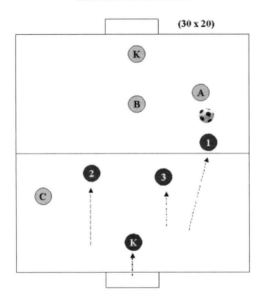

Diagram 34

1. Introduce **offside** from the half way line but only with players old enough to grasp the concept .You need to judge this for yourself. This will help create a situation where, when the team win the ball and take it forward, the concept of pushing up from the back **(compactness)** can come into place. Note that the team can create compact-ness from the back even when the opposition have the ball. For instance, when the defending team force the attacking team to play the ball back and / or keep pressure on the ball to prevent a forward pass.

2. Before offside was introduced (C) could have stayed in the position above and received a pass if (A) won the ball. This may have affected (2)'s position even though that team had the ball as (2) may have felt obliged to position in only a semi - attacking position should their team lose the ball.

3. Now it is more realistic as (C) would be offside should (A) win the ball and pass it, so (2) can push up and leave (C)

free, knowing that should possession change, (C) is offside.

COMPACTNESS

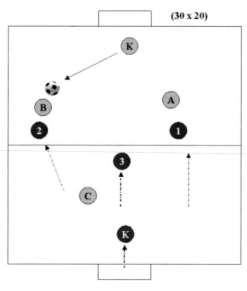

(30 x 20)

Diagram 35

1.   Here we show how we can get compactness throughout the team even while the opposition has possession of the ball.

2.   This is particularly effective if there is pressure on the ball and the opponent has possession but is facing his own goal.

3.   This means effectively that they can't pass the ball forward and this gives our players the chance to squeeze up from the back. As a consequence they can, in this situation, leave one of the opponents in an offside position and out of the game.

4.   If the player is allowed to turn and face forward and have the opportunity to pass the ball forward the other players aren't able to move forward as effectively.

5.   Hence the pressuring player is vitally important in this process and must do a good job of preventing the forward pass, forcing the player to pass back, or win back the ball if possible.

GETTING IT WRONG

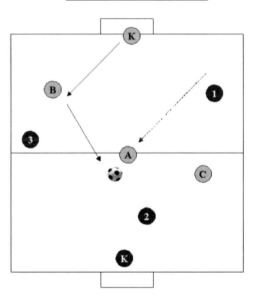

Diagram 36

1.   (3) should press the ball to make it difficult for (B) but doesn't do so. Therefore, (B) has time and space to play and keep possession. Here there is an easy pass to (A) who is in a very dangerous attacking position.

2.   (A) makes a forward diagonal run to receive a pass. (1) has the responsibility to either recover back behind the ball or track the run of (A) to prevent him from getting free to receive the pass. By not doing this (A) is free to receive the pass and threaten (2) who now has a 2 v 1 against.

3. It just takes a lack of effort by a player to make it very difficult for teammates who are then drawn out of position to try to compensate.

4. In defending it is imperative that all players function together as a unit to be successful.

FREE PLAY

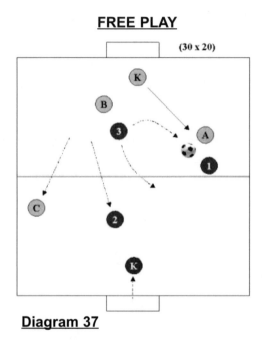

(30 x 20)

Diagram 37

1. The numbers team have attacked and shot at goal, the keeper makes a save.

2. The keeper passes to (A) who is then **pressured** by (1).

3. Player (3), who was in the attack, makes a **recovery run** to help (1) by getting back into an inside **support** position.

4. An option for (3) is to **double up** with (1) to attack and pressurize (A) from opposite sides.

5. Player (C) makes a forward run that (2) successfully **tracks**.

Note, (2)'s tracking back run is not with (C) but back into a position to provide balanced cover for (1) and (3) while at the same time keeping an eye on (C). It could be argued this is more like a recovery run but it is based initially on the movement of (C).

When the defending team regain possession and move the ball forward to attack the opponent's goal, the team can move forward (creating **compactness**) and the keeper can move up to fill the space left to act as a keeper / sweeper.

CHAPTER FOUR

DEFENDING IN a 4 v 4 SMALL - SIDED GAME

ESTABLISHING THE ESSENTIAL KEY COACHING POINTS IN DEFENDING USING THE 4 v 4 MODEL

BASIC SHAPE OF a 4 v 4 HIGHLIGHTING THE KEY COACHING POINTS

4 v 4: THE BASIC DIAMOND / KITE SHAPE

As in the three v three games, the reward for the defending team winning the ball is a chance to score a goal but they must do it within 5 passes of regaining possession. If this isn't achieved, start again with the team trying to win the ball again through good defending principles.

Ultimately have a 4 v 4 small sided game letting, them play free with no restrictions.

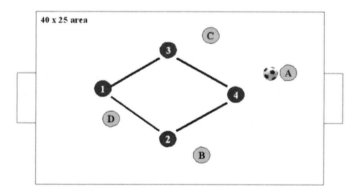

Diagram 38

1.   The main idea here is for the defending team to **condense** the area the ball can be played into, the defending team becomes a diamond **within** the opponents attacking diamond. (4) forces (A) one way and the

rest of the team adjust their positions off this. (3) protects
the **space inside** but can **close down** (C) if the ball is
passed, (2) and (1) do the same and this results
in the defending diamond being **shorter** and **tighter**.

2.   As the opponents move, the defending team must move
to compensate. Also, if any pass is played in behind players (1) (2) or (3) they should be first to the ball.

3.   **<u>Coaching Points</u>**

a) **Pressure** – 1 v 1 defending to win the ball, delay or
force a bad pass.
b) **Support** – position of immediate teammate (angle, distance and communication).
c) **Cover / Balance**– positions of teammates beyond the
supporting player.
d) **Recovering and Tracking** should the ball go past our
position, recovery run to goal side of the ball and tracking
the run of a player.
e) **Double Teaming** – here two players attack the player
on the ball from two sides.
f) **Compactness** from the back (pushing up as a unit)
particularly on **Regaining Possession.**

4.   The objectives of defending are to **disrupt** the other
team's build up, make play **predictable**, **prevent** forward
passes and ultimately **regain** possession of the ball.

5.   Techniques include – pressuring, marking, tackling and
winning the ball.

PRESSURE AND SUPPORT

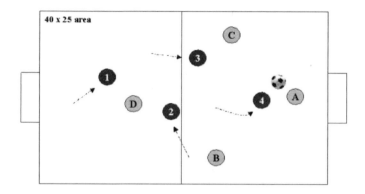

Diagram 39

1.   (4) presses and forces (A) outside. (3) adjusts position to get into a support position to help (4) and at the same time shadow (C).

2.   The diamond or kite shape is still maintained by the defending team but it is a smaller one within the larger attacking team's diamond.

3.   A progression could be to play **offside** from the half way line. You can start the play without including offside (as we did in the 3 v 3's) until the players get comfortable in the set up. Go through all the coaching points within the session before moving to this.

4.   Again, when working with very young players, be careful not to introduce offside situations before they are ready, as the concept is difficult for them to understand. It is up to you to be able to recognize when they are ready.

COVER / BALANCE

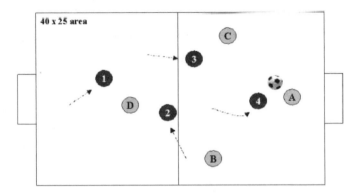

Diagram 40

1.   The players beyond and behind the pressuring player (4) and the supporting player (3) offer cover and balance to the team.

2.   (2) pushes across to fill a central space where the ball is likely to be played. (B) is unlikely to receive a pass because of the angle. (4) has closed (A) down so (2) marks space more. (2) is still aware of (B) and positions to be able to see the ball and his immediate opponent (B).

3.   (1) pushes forward and across, again to fill a potential passing space based on where (4) is showing (A) on the ball. At the same time he must be aware of (D)'s position.

4.   (1) maintains depth to cover for any ball being played over the top and behind, particularly if (A) is able to play the ball forward.

5.   If (4) does a good pressuring job on (A) to prevent a forward pass then (1) can adjust position accordingly, knowing a ball can't be played in behind. This would mean being able to take up a position that isn't as deep in relation to where (D) is.

RECOVERY RUNS

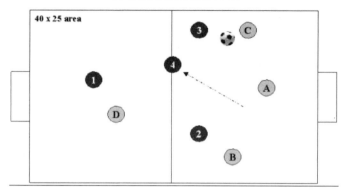

40 x 25 area

Diagram 41

1.   (3) is isolated in a 1 v 1 situation in a wide area of the field.(D) and (B) have positioned away from the area of the ball to affect the positions of defenders (1) and (2).

2.   (4) makes a recovery run back into a supporting position to help (3).

3.   Should the ball be passed back to (A) then (4) can push forward again to apply pressure to the ball.

4.   Recovering back behind the ball makes the defending team stronger and forms a greater barrier for the attacking team.

5.   This is good team play by (4) to recover back to help. Players need to work unselfishly, particularly when defending.

6.   It could be argued that (4) could stay at the front of the diamond to mark (A) but that leaves (3) exposed. By working back, (4) is now doing four jobs instead of only one; recovering goal side of the ball, supporting (3), covering any movement by (A) and in this instance positioning in the passing lane to try to stop a pass to (D).

TRACKING

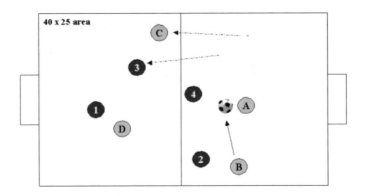

Diagram 42

1.   Here (C) makes a run to escape defender (3) and help (A) on the ball. The defender (3) has to track this run to ensure (C) doesn't get free.

2.   Tracking opponents is not a fun part of the game for players but nevertheless is a very important part of defending successfully.

3.   (C) is unlikely to receive a pass as (3) has done a very good tracking job and given (A) one less option on the ball. (3) has also got into a good position on the goal side of (C).

DOUBLE TEAMING

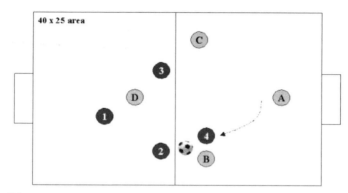

Diagram 43

1. While recovering back behind the ball to support the player strengthens the defensive set up of the defending team, a more aggressive defensive movement is high-lighted here.

2. (4) has worked back to close down (B) on the ball from a different angle to the first pressuring player (2).

3. It is best if (4) can close down (B) in a curved run, cutting off the pass back to (A) along the passing lane that was available previously as an outlet pass for (B).

4. This puts the defending team in a very strong position to win back the ball, but the movement must be made quickly to give (B) very little time to get out of trouble.

5. To further support winning the ball back, (2) has forced (B) inside and (1) and (3) have positioned ball side of their immediate opponents to fill the spaces available around the ball to ensure they are first to it should it be passed.

6. Doubling up like this can win the ball but at worst, if they don't win it, then between them, (2) and (4) closing quickly enough could force an error by (B).

DOUBLE TEAMING

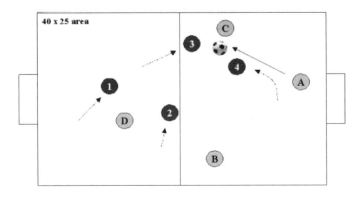

Diagram 44

1.   All previous coaching points apply.

2.   Introduce **double teaming** in a 4 v 4 e.g. (4) doubles up
        with (3) to pressurize (B). (4) closes down (B) with a
        curved run to cut off the passing lane back to (A). (3)
        forces (B) inside to the strength of the defending team.
        Try to prevent the pass from (B) to (D) which is the obvi-
        ous way out for the attacking team to keep possession.

3.   All players compress towards the ball, marking space
        while keeping their immediate opponents in full view and
        within closing distance should the ball be played to them.
        The closer they are to the ball the more they mark oppo-
        nents, the further away from the ball the more they mark
        space.

4.   Players work in a diamond or kite shape. The defending
        team's diamond is shorter and tighter than the attacking
        team's diamond, almost a diamond within a diamond. This
        is designed to close down the spaces around and in the
        immediate vicinity of the ball but also in relation to the
        positions of the opposition's players.

DEFENDING IN a 4 v 4 SITUATION

DOUBLE TEAMING

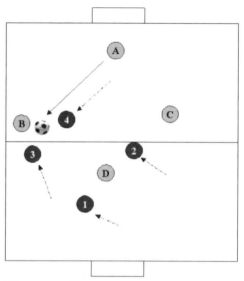

Diagram 45

1.   All previous coaching points apply.

2.   Introduce **double teaming** in a 4 v 4 e.g. (4) doubles up
        with (3) to pressurize (B). (4) closes down (B) with a
        curved run to cut off the passing lane back to (A). (3)
        forces (B) inside to the strength of the defending team.
        Try to prevent the pass from (B) to (D) which is the obvi-
        ous way out for the attacking team to keep possession.

3.   All players compress towards the ball, marking space but
        keeping their immediate opponents in full view and within
        closing distance should the ball be played to them. The
        closer they are to the ball the more they mark opponents,
        the further away from the ball the more they mark space.

4.   Players work in a diamond or kite shape. The defending
        team's diamond is shorter and tighter than the attacking
        team's diamond, almost a diamond within a diamond. This

is designed to close down the spaces around and in the immediate vicinity of the ball but also in relation to the positions of the opposition's players.

COMPACTNESS

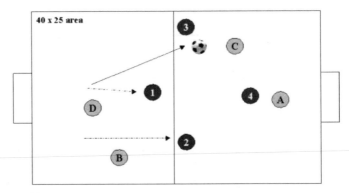

Diagram 46

1.   (1) wins the ball and passes it forward to (3) who maintains possession.

2.   On winning possession it is up to the defenders to push up the field and get into supporting positions for their teammates, creating **compactness** from the back.

3.   In the above example, (D) and (B) have pushed on to support their previous attack, lost the ball to (1) and not tracked the runs of (1) and (2) forward.

4.   This creates two points of interest if using the offside rule: both (D) and (B) are left offside by the movement forward of (1) and (2) but also the numbers team now have a 4 v 2 situation in their favor.

5.   This is particularly effective if the movement forward is done quickly once it is established that (3) has comfort-able possession of the ball, as it may catch (D) and (B) off-guard.

FREE PLAY

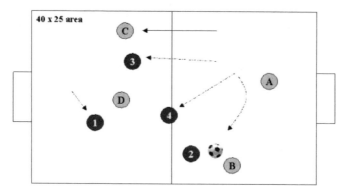

Diagram 47

1. The **Pressure** on the ball from (2) forces (B) inside.

2. A **Recovery run** is made by (4) to get into a **support** position to help (2).

3. Other option as shown could be for (4) to be more aggressive and **double up** on (B) to help (2).

4. **Balance** is created at the back by (1) marking the space inside the striker (D) but also covering for (2) and (4).

5. A **tracking run** is made by (3), shadowing (C) who has broken forward.

6.   This shows all the players working together as a team.

7. Final key point would be if the defending team successfully won back possession of the ball they would move up the field as a team, getting **compactness** from the back.

8. As mentioned, they can also get compact by moving up even when the opponents have the ball and can't play it forward due to pressure or pass it back. But the best time to do it is when the defending team regain possession and they can dictate the moment.

9.   Within this movement of the players we have shown all the key coaching points of defending being used effectively by the defending team to glve them the best chance of regaining possession of the ball.

GETTING IT WRONG

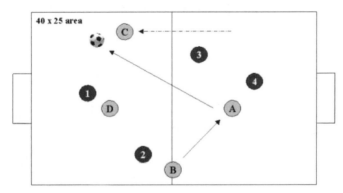

Diagram 48

1.   Here we see (B) passing to (A) and with no recovery run back by (4) to put pressure on the ball (A) can pick out teammates easily with passes.

2.   (C) has made a great forward run and (3) has not tracked this run which leaves the numbers team exposed at the back.

3.   (1) is now faced with a 2 v 1 against and (A) will have pushed up to add further support.

4.   By players not making the required defensive adjustments the defending team now look likely to concede a goal.

5.   It only takes a moment's lack of concentration by a player or players to result in opponents getting into dangerous scoring situations. Here (1) is in an almost impossible defensive situation to prevent the opponents from scoring a goal.

CHAPTER FIVE

DEFENDING IN 6 v 6 SMALL SIDED GAMES.

HOW TO PRESENT A SMALL - SIDED GAME

This is a game of less than 11 v 11 that can be any number from 3 v 3 to 9 v 9. The general sizes of a game to establish **team** coaching themes are usually 6 v 6 or 8 v 8. I have included two examples of set ups for these games.

Session Plan

a)   Only coach one team at a time.

b)   Try to work with **all** the players on the team you are coaching, affecting each performance in a positive way.

c)   Stay with one theme / topic at a time. Don't jump from one to another during the session. Tthis will only confuse the players.

d)   Divide the field into thirds; defending, middle, attacking, for easier points of reference. Use cones to show the boundaries.

e)   Use specific start positions to get the session going.

f)   Develop your theme using the key coaching points and check you have covered them in the session.

g)   List the key points in the order you perceive them in the process of building the session. For example, in defending, pressure on the ball comes before support. Once you let the game go free, key points can be highlighted in any order depending on if the previous key point was performed correctly and didn't need to be addressed.

h)   Move from simple to complex as you develop the session. For example, in the theme **defending from the front,** coach individual play within the team concept first (working with one striker), move to coaching a unit of players (it could be the two strikers working together), then extend the numbers (maybe working with the strikers and midfield players then finish with coaching the whole team (strikers, midfielders, defenders, keeper).

i) You may work the other way around depending on your session theme. For example, if your session is **playing from the back,** you could start with the distribution of the ball from the keeper (individual) to working with a wide defender receiving from the keeper (individual) developing the theme with each individual defender. Then move onto the defending unit and the keeper combined (unit) then introduce the midfield players (combined units) and finally the strikers (whole team).

j) This is individual - unit - team; in this order building up the session from simple to complex in a logical order.

k) This is just an example of how it can be done in a logical order; it is up to the individual coach to develop his own method to suit his own style of coaching.

l) Once the defending team have won back the ball they have 5 passes (or whatever the coach decides) to score a goal. Then the game restarts with the defending team having to win back the ball again. This is because we are working on defending and don't want the team to spend a lot of time with the ball on attacking play. By giving them the chance to attack once they have won the ball they have a reward for good defending.

<u>THE 6 v 6 SMALL SIDED GAME PLAN SET UP</u>

All 6 v 6 games can use offside from the defending thirds, but as previously discussed, depending on the players, you can introduce offside at the appropriate time. For this chapter we are using offside for all the plans.

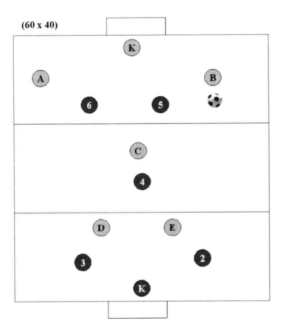

<u>Diagram 49</u>

1.   The above set up is a 6 v 6 (2-1-2) with the field divided into thirds for easier points of reference; defending, midfield and attacking thirds.

2.   Play offside from the edge of the defending third to keep the game realistic, though you could start without this condition to help the players ease into the session.

3.   Each stage of the session can be described as a **progression** or **development** from the last one and you can clearly list this in your session plan to help you.

START POSITIONS FOR DEFENDING
IN A SMALL SIDED GAME

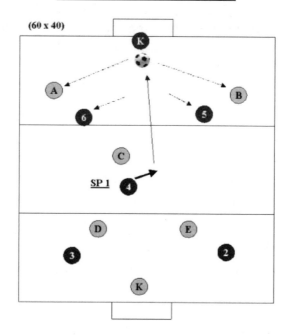

Diagram 50

1. (4) moves the ball with a touch to signify the beginning of the practice and shoots at goal. The keeper collects the ball and the defenders break wide to receive in space.

2. Working on defending from the front, midfield, then the back can be the sequence, or you can do it the other way around and work from the back, the midfield then the front.

3. If from the front using the strikers (5) and (6) as first defenders the keeper begins the movement with a pass or throw to the defenders (A) or (B). If from the back the keeper begins the movement with a pass or throws to the front players (D) or (E) and you coach players (2) and (3) to begin.

4. You can condition the keeper to throw to certain players to keep control of the session and ensure you build it the way you want it to go. For example, to start from the front have the keeper throw or pass the ball to back players (A) and (B) alternately. Next throw or pass the ball to player (C) in midfield, and then finally throw or pass the ball to strikers (D) and (E) alternately. At each stage you can work with the relevant defending players and what they should do to win the ball back.

5. The session plans are presented as a full team but you can break them down and concentrate on a unit at a time and eventually take it to the full team set up as shown.

6. Make sure the players you work with in each unit get all the concepts correct before moving on to the next unit. For example, strikers (5) and (6) have to understand their defensive priorities before you move to the midfield player and so on.

DEFENDING IN a 6 v 6 SITUATION SHOWING OUTSIDE

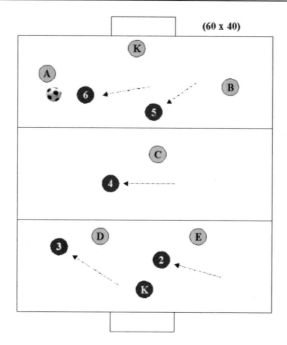

Diagram 51

Playing offside from the 20 yard line at each end (defensive third). All previous coaching points apply. Introduce getting **compact** from the back. Playing offside from the thirds trains the players' minds to start to develop this aspect of play. The defending team makes play predictable by forcing play down one route.

Key factors of Defending are:

a) **Pressure** (Keeping play in front, delaying or winning the ball).

b) **Support** (Angle / Distance / Communication).

c) **Cover / Balance** (marking zones and / or players).

d) **Recover** (getting goal side of the ball).

e) **Tracking** (opponent's runs).

f) **Double teaming** and **triple teaming** (2 or 3 players closing down the same player on the ball from different angles).

g) **Regaining Possession** and **Compactness** (on regaining possession, players push out from the back).

SHOWING INSIDE

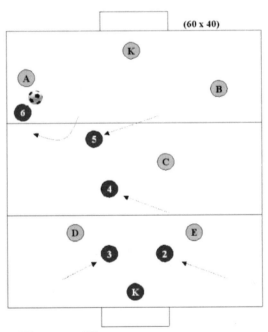

(60 x 40)

Diagram 52

1. (6) shows inside to numbers, stops the pass down the line and players adjust accordingly. Try to force (A) to play across to (B) and give (5) a chance to intercept.

2. (4) supports (6), covers (C) and screens the pass (marks space) into the front men ready to intercept.

3. (5) could even double team with (6), closing at an angle so the pass to (B) is screened.

PRESSURE AND SUPPORT

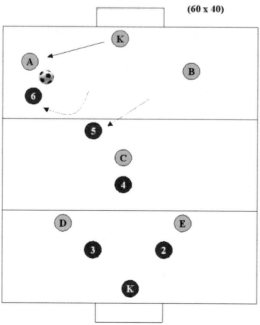

Diagram 53

1.   You can work the session getting all the key points in by setting up to defend from the front. The structure is as follows: Work with, in order, a) the front two players, b) the midfield player, c) the two defenders, d) the team as a whole.

2.   Work with (5) and (6) on **pressure** and **support**. The keeper plays the ball to (A) who has broken wide to receive the pass. Work with (6) on pressuring the ball. If possible (6) can show the player inside to the support position of (5) who must support (6) and screen (B) at the same time.

3.   Work both sides having (B) receive a pass from the keeper also and this time have (5) pressure and (6) support. If they win the ball between them they can immediately attack on goal (this is what they are trying to achieve).

FULL TEAM ADJUSTMENT

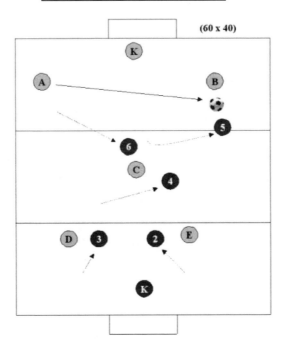

Diagram 54

1.   Here (A) has been forced to play the ball across the field to (B) by the positioning of the team preventing a penetrating pass forward.

2.   The diagram above shows the team adjustment across the field to compensate for this and how they try to prevent the attacking team from getting forward down the other side of the field.

3.   (5)'s first action should be to try to intercept the pass. If this isn't successful then at least put pressure on (B).

4.   If (5) can force the player inside, the above shape takes place. (4) can still get close to pressure (C) and mark the space at the same time. (6) can close down (A) if the ball is played back (or even intercept the pass with good anticipation) but also double up with (4) should it be played into midfield to (C).

FULL TEAM ADJUSTMENT

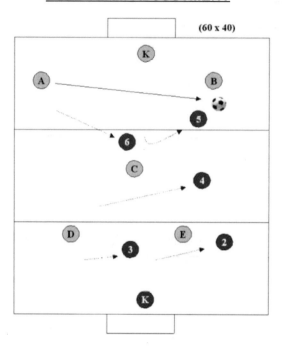

(60 x 40)

Diagram 55

1.   If (5) can't get across to force (B) inside then (2) shows the biggest adjustment, marking the other side of (E) as that is where the pass is likely to be made. This is marking the outside space instead of the inside space as (5)'s position would prevent a pass into that space.

2.   (4) moves across further but still aware of (C), and (3) changes position again, moving across to the area the ball is likely to be played into.

3.   Everyone's position is affected, depending on where the pressing player (5) forces the ball to go, in this case down the side of the field (in the previous case back into the middle).

COVER / BALANCE

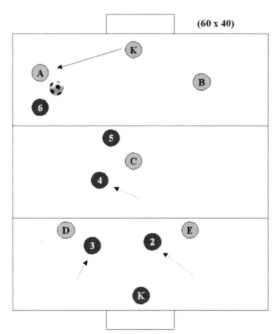

Diagram 56

1. Dealing with the positioning of the players who are beyond the pressuring and supporting players of the team who provide **balance** and **cover**.

2. Here (6) forces the pass inside so (4) covers the likely space the ball can be played into while at the same time being aware of (C)'s position should he receive a pass.

3. (2) and (3) come together into the positions where the ball is likely to be played while at the same time being aware of their defensive responsibilities regarding (D) and (E).

RECOVERY RUNS

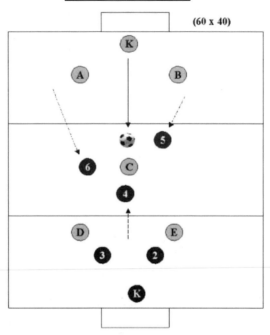

(60 x 40)

Diagram 57

1.   Here the keeper plays the ball to the midfield player who is then pressured by (4).

2.   You will work on the pressuring of (4) as a matter of course and how (3) and (2) support and cover depending on which way (4) shows the player.

3.   Work can now be with the two strikers (5) and (6) who must **recover** back to help (4). They can recover back behind the ball as above with (6), or with (5), slightly in front to get into the passing lane to prevent a pass to (B). (6) gets goal-side to force (C) to pass back to (A) and then (6) pressures (A) with the pass to (B) already cut off by (5)'s position.

4.   Hence we have two situations; recovering **behind** the ball and recovering in **front** of the ball, both limiting the options of (C) on the ball.

TRACKING PLAYERS' RUNS

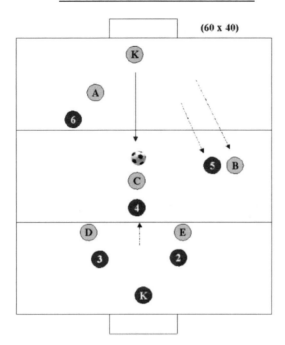

Diagram 58

1. Here (B) has taken the initiative and made a forward run
    to help (C). If (B) is allowed to go free then the defending
    team is very vulnerable down that side of the field. If (5)
    does not track the runner it poses a problem for (2) who is
    the nearest defender to the ball: Does (2) mark (E) or
    close down (B)?

2. Above, (5) has **tracked** the run of (B), showing how
    important it is for strikers to realize they are the first line of
    defense in the team. Hence we have created a situation
    to show how another key coaching point has been prac-
    ticed in the game.

3. The coach has to identify this situation and coach it. It
    may be that (5) didn't see the run of (B) or track it and this
    is a chance for the coach to affect (5)'s positioning by
    stopping the play and coaching the fault.

DOUBLE TEAMING AND TRIPLE TEAMING

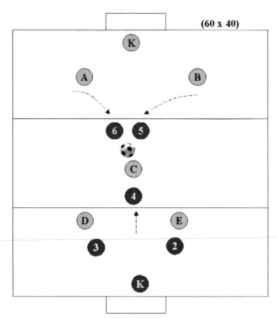

Diagram 59

1.   Here (5) has taken it a step further with a recovery run into a **double teaming** position, attacking and pressuring (C) from the other side, thus creating a better chance of winning the ball.

2.   If the players can react quickly enough, you could have a **triple teaming** situation also with (6) closing down from another angle.

3.   The recovery runs into double / triple team positions can be along the lines (passing lanes) of the passes back to (A) and (B), making it very difficult for (C) to escape with the ball.

CONDENSING PLAY CREATING COMPACTNESS

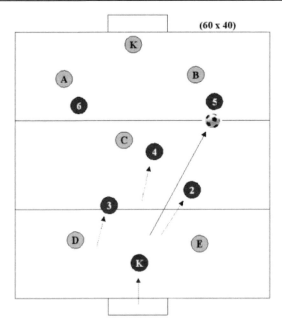

Diagram 60

1. Here (2) has won the ball back in the defending third and played it forward. The whole team has moved forward creating **compactness** from the back, leaving the opposing strikers offside and making themselves available to receive a pass should the ball need to be passed backwards.

2. Finally, let the game go free and have the keeper play the ball to any player on the team and coach the faults as they occur during the game with all the key coaching points of defending in mind.

3. To make sure you work consistently with the defending team, allow them only a restricted number of passes to work a position to shoot at goal. Then the ball goes back to the other team as we want to work on defending and not attacking. Maybe give them six passes maximum to score after regaining possession of the ball.

CONDENSING PLAY CREATING COMPACTNESS

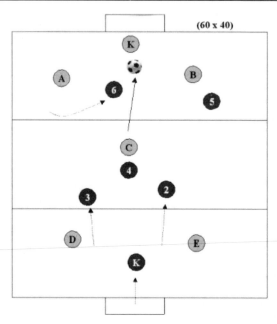

Diagram 61

1.   This is an example to show that the defending team do not only move forward when they regain possession of the ball but can do so even when the opponents have the ball in their possession. Good pressure by (4) has stopped (C) from passing the ball forward. (5) and (6) position to prevent the pass back to (A) or (B). The only option is a pass all the way back to the keeper. This longer pass gives defenders (2) and (3) time to move forward and as a consequence leave (D) and (E) offside. The defending keeper moves up also to cover for the defenders (keeper – sweeper).

2.   (6) anticipates the back pass and produces more good pressure, this time on the keeper, which may result in winning the ball back. Should the keeper kick and clear the ball long, the movement in the meantime of the back players will cause the attacking team's opponents to be offside from this clearance.

SHOWING ALL KEY COACHING POINTS

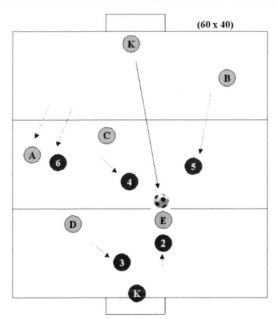

Diagram 62

1. Now have the keeper play the ball into the strikers and work on the defenders (2) and (3), pressuring and supporting, bringing in the other key coaching points as they happen. Above are examples of what can happen with the defending team's players; (2) **presses** the ball, (3) drops into a **support** position, (5) starts a **recovery run**, (6) **tracks** the forward run of (A), (4) **doubles up** on (E) to help (2) win the ball back or at least try to force (E) into making an error and losing the ball.

2. Finally, once the defending team win the ball back they obviously will look to play the ball forward at the earliest option and this will result in the team moving up the field from the back and the defenders at least getting up to the offside line at the limit of the defending third (this is called **condensing play** from the back, which creates **compactness**).

FREE PLAY

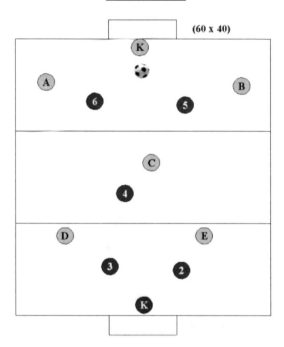

Diagram 63

1.   Finally, after working through the team with the keeper throwing or passing the ball to each unit in turn (defenders, midfield, attackers), to ensure the defending team get a chance to defend in each third of the field and each key coaching point can be covered, it is time to let the game go free.

2.   Now the keeper has the option of throwing or passing to any player on the attacking team and the defending players have to act accordingly.

3.   As a coach it is time to identify the fault (see the **coaching moment** as it happens) and correct it. The defending team work to try to win the ball and score a goal as quickly as possible, then the ball goes back to the attacking team and the coach works with the defending team again, constantly reinforcing the defensive theme.

4.   Within the open game there will be occasions to correct play using all the key coaching points both individually, as a unit and as a team.

GETTING IT WRONG

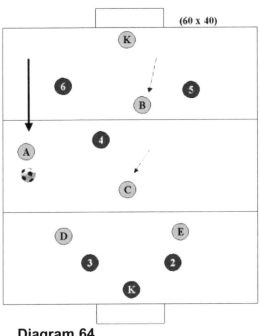

(60 x 40)

Diagram 64

These are obvious mistakes that players can make based on the key points in defending and are used to highlight situations that can easily go wrong.

1.   The numbers team have attacked and shot at goal and been caught going forward. The opponents catch them out with a quick break. (A) starts the move after a pass from the keeper and (6) **doesn't track** the run.

2.   Now we have a situation where (A) has **no pressure** and is free to play. No pressure on the ball means the strikers (D) and (E) can push (3) and (2) **deeper** to create more space in front for (A) and (C) to play in.

3.   (4) **doesn't recover back** to get goal-side so (C) is open
        to receive a pass in lots of space and time.

4.   Other principles cannot now be applied; there is no
        pressure so there is **no support**.

5.   There is **no cover** at the back because of the overloaded
        situation.

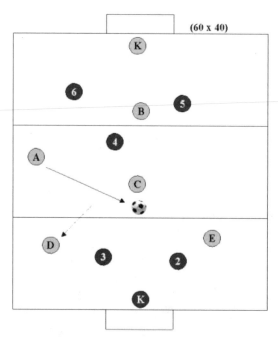

Diagram 65

6.   This is now a 4 v 2 against and (3) has to decide whether
        to stay and mark (D) or attack the ball and leave (D) free.

7.   The correct defensive principles have not been applied at
        the start of the move, putting the other players in very dif-
        ficult positions. For example does (3) track and mark (D)
        or close down (C)?

8.   (3) closes (C), then (D) is free to receive a pass and
        shoot. (2) closes and (E) is free. (3) stays with (D) and (C)
        is free to shoot and so on.

9. This serves as an example of what can happen when teams do not defend properly and it's likely with such an overloaded situation that the defending team will concede a goal or at least have to give up a shot at goal.

CHAPTER SIX

8 v 8 DEFENDING IN A SMALL-SIDED GAME

8 v 8 SMALL SIDED GAME PLAN SET UP

Working offside from the defending thirds

As previously discussed in smaller sided games, when the defending team win back the ball offer them the reward for this with the chance to score a goal against their opponents but restrict them to 5 passes or less to ensure concentration is still on the principles of defending play not attacking play.

The game restarts again when they have, or have not, scored a goal within 5 passes after winning possession of the ball.

Ultimately open the game up to free play with no restrictions.

DETERMINING THE ESSENTIAL KEY COACHING POINTS IN DEFENDING USING THE 8 v 8 MODEL

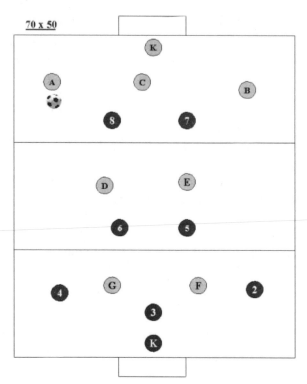

Diagram 66

1.   Here the set up is a 3 – 2 – 2 which provides overloads
      at each end of the field with 3 v 2's in the favor of the
      defending team.

2.   You can use any set up you want but this is the most
      logical one with these numbers of players available
      because it provides a realistic game situation as defend-
      ers in the defending third generally have the upper hand
      on numbers against the strikers and in the midfield third
      there are usually equal numbers.

DEFENDING IN AN 8 v 8 SITUATION

Work with the two strikers first then the two midfield players, and finally the three defenders. Condition the opponent's keeper to serve to defenders then midfield then strikers. In each phase work each unit one at a time (strikers, midfielders and defenders), then let it go free and coach the faults as they happen. The same principles apply as in the 6 v 6.

HIGH PRESSURE AND SUPPORT SHOWING INSIDE

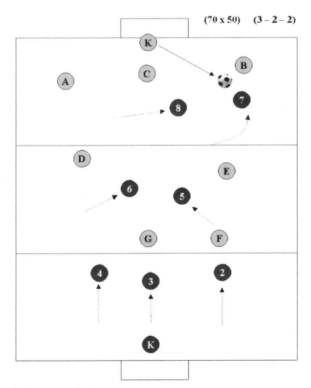

(70 x 50)   (3 – 2 – 2)

Diagram 67

1.   Full team high pressure starting from quick pressure from the first defender (7).

2.   (7) makes a curved run to force (B) to pass the ball inside into the strength and numbers of the defending team and

cut off the outside route to (E) or (F), taking both these players out of the game by this positioning alone.

3.   (8) takes up a supporting position inside but ready to close down (C) should (B) look to pass.

4.   (5) and (6) can position inside to where the ball is being forced to go.

5.   (2), (3), and (4) take the opportunity to push up as (7) has stopped the immediate forward pass, allowing them to get compactness from the back.

HIGH PRESSURE AND SUPPORT SHOWING OUTSIDE

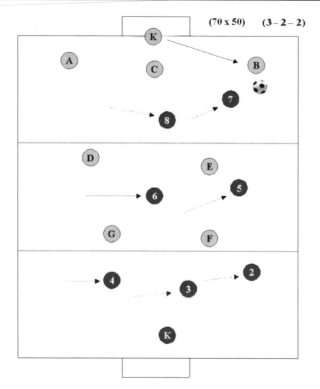

(70 x 50)   (3 – 2 – 2)

Diagram 68

1.   **Forwards**: (7) shows down the line, (8) supports across. This forces (B) to play the ball down the line.

2.   **Midfield**: (5) moves outside the shoulder of (E), (6) supports across (covering positions).

3.   **Defenders**: (2) moves outside the shoulder of (F), covering a quick counter-attack down the wing. (3) and (4) support across

4.   If the ball is played to (E), (5) and (7) or (8) can double team. Players recover and track as the ball goes past them.

LOW PRESSURE AND SUPPORT

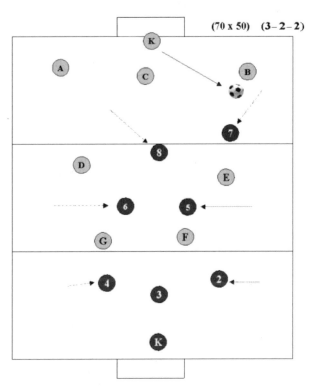

(70 x 50) (3–2–2)

Diagram 69

1.   When the closest player can't close early enough he should stay in position, not close down and invite the opposition to try to play through.

2. Close the spaces up behind to make it difficult for the other team to pass through you. Be patient and force them to play to where you are strong.

3. (8) drops off and across the field and (7) holds position and is ready to pounce should the ball be brought forward and into tackling distance.

4. This is a more patient approach and may be used against a team who are very good technically at the back and able to play through a high pressuring team, so we invite them onto us and keep it tight behind the ball as a team to reduce the space they have to play in.

COVER / BALANCE

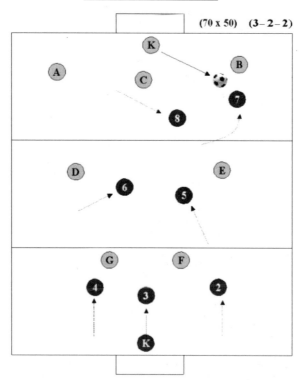

Diagram 70

1. Behind the work of (7) and (8), (5) and (6) provide cover and balance to help them win the ball back.

2. They move into the spaces where the ball is being forced to go while at the same time being aware of the positions of their immediate opponents (D) and (E).

3. (4), (3) and (2) use the opportunity to push out and again offer cover and balance to the team's position.

RECOVERY RUNS

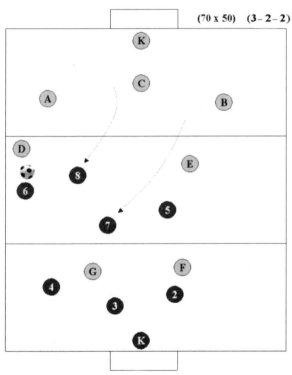

Diagram 71

1. Here the numbers team may have attacked and lost the ball and must recover back into positions to help the team defend.

2.   (6) pressures (D) on the ball. (4), (3), and (2) get into good cover / balancing positions behind the ball. (5) Is focusing on (E). (7) and (8) both make important recovery runs to overload the situation around the area of the ball.

3.   The main points of recovering back are: the players making the runs must consider how far back they run, not going too deep or not going far enough as to be ineffective. Here (8) could drop a little deeper to become the support player for (6), and (7) has retreated to a good covering / balancing position. If the defending team doesn't win the ball it may be they force (D) to pass back and this helps the defending team move up the field away from their goal.

TRACKED RUNS

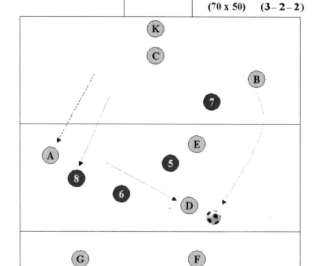

(70 x 50)   (3 – 2 – 2)

<u>Diagram 72</u>

1.   Above are examples of an effective tracking run and what happens when a player doesn't make the required run.

2.   Tracking runs, as discussed, are a very important part of the game. (A) makes a forward run and is tracked effectively by (8). (D) makes a diagonal run but (6) doesn't track the run. This makes it easy for (B) to play a forward pass to (D) into the free space.

3.   Players need to be particularly astute at covering these types of runs in the midfield area of the field. If (6) makes the required tracking run to mark (D) then (B)'s passing options are limited.

DOUBLE TEAMING

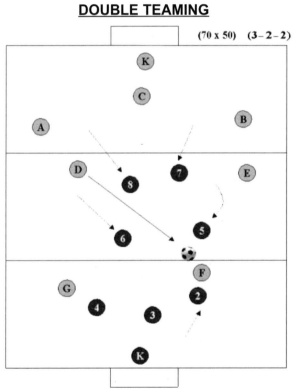

(70 x 50)   (3 – 2 – 2)

Diagram 73

1.   (D) gets free from (6) and plays a forward pass to (F) coming short to receive. (2) pressures from behind to prevent (F) from turning and (5) leaves (E) to double up from the other side. (5) makes a run along the passing lane of (E) to cut off a potential escape route for (F).

2.   This results in (F) only being able to pass inside and (6)
        moves back and across ready to triple team if the chance
        arises but at least into a position to intercept a possible
        pass by (F). (8) and (7) can help by making recovery runs
        into other open spaces around the ball. A pass to (G) is
        likely to be intercepted by (4).

COMPACTNESS

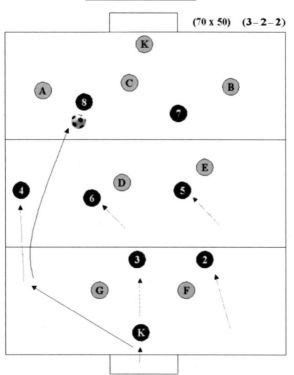

Diagram 74

1.   In this example the keeper has gained possession of the
        ball and thrown it to (4), who passes it forward to (8) in
        the attacking third. This is a great opportunity for the
        whole team to move forward and get **compactness**
        throughout the team starting from the back. As a conse-
        quence, the opponent's strikers are left offside and have
        to work back themselves.

2.   Don't forget, the defending team can achieve compactness also when the opponents have the ball, such as
when the attacking team are prevented from playing a
forward pass by good pressure or are forced to pass the
ball back, particularly over a bigger distance, which gives
more time for the forward movement to happen.

FREE PLAY

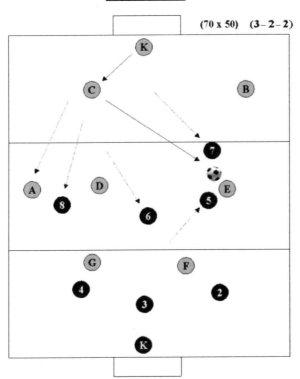

(70 x 50)   (3 – 2 – 2)

Diagram 75

1.   The numbers team have made an attack and shot at goal.
The keeper passes the ball to (C) who passes to midfielder (E).

2.   (5) **pressures** the ball, (6) takes up a **support** position
with a **recovery run** back behind the ball, (2), (3), and (4)
take up good **covering** positions in respect to where the
ball is and where (F) and (G) are, (8) **tracks** (A)'s forward

run and (7) drops back to **double up** on (E) to help
pressuring player (5).

3.   Should they win the ball back, the defending team will
move forward to gain **compactness** from the back.

GETTING IT WRONG

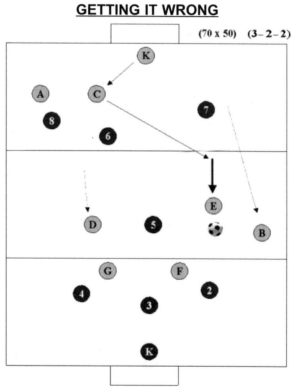

(70 x 50)   (3–2–2)

Diagram 76

1.   These are examples to highlight the types of problems
that can occur in association with the key coaching points
of defending. This shows what can happen when the
team does not make the necessary adjustments on
defense. The numbers team have attacked and shot at
goal. The keeper makes a save and passes to (C).
Midfielder (6) is caught going forward from the previous
attack and is out of position defensively.

2.   (5) **doesn't pressure** so (E) receives and turns to be free to attack. (6) **doesn't recover** back so (D) is unmarked. (7) **doesn't track** (B)'s run so (B) is free in a dangerous position also. We now have a 5 v 4 in the favor of the attacking team and the defensive team is **overloaded** and in a very weak position because players have not done their defensive duties. (2) is exposed in almost a 3 v 1 against. This is an extreme example but shows what can happen if the team does not defend properly.

PRESSURIZING GAME IN AN 8 v 8

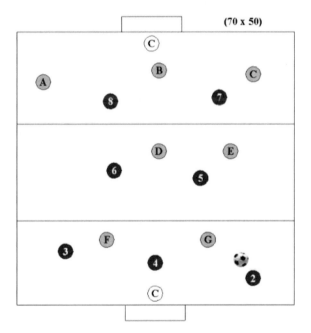

(70 x 50)

Diagram 77

1.   The game is designed to work on **pressurizing** the player on the ball, **prevent** a forward pass and ultimately win the ball. Closest player has to pressure the ball.

2.   To score, a player has to make a pass from **anywhere** into the coach (or a keeper or designated target player). The ball can be played in the air to the target's hands (to

practice quality long distance lofted passes) or on the ground to feet (driven passes). All over the field players must work hard to close the ball down quickly.

3.   **Develop** – A) As a reward, when a team scores a goal they keep possession so they play to the opposite goal to score. Previously they played to the same goal and the opposition got the ball when they scored. B) Go to **man – marking** so in possession players must get free and defenders must work hard to keep them from scoring.

4.   Show by **high pressure** as a team how defenders can win the ball back early and close to the opponent's goal to score. The team must push up from the back to start this.

5.   You can use different numbers of players to play this game and different sizes of fields. Also you can perform the game without goalkeepers where the players have to chip or drive the ball into the empty goal. They can do this from anywhere as in the above game and can score within one pass.

6.   Have some fun with it and perhaps introduce the idea that if the closest player doesn't close his opponent down and that opponent scores by getting the ball to the target then the defender has to perform 3 push ups. It is particularly obvious who is at fault from a defensive aspect when we do the man for man marking game. This highlights to all the players who was at fault.

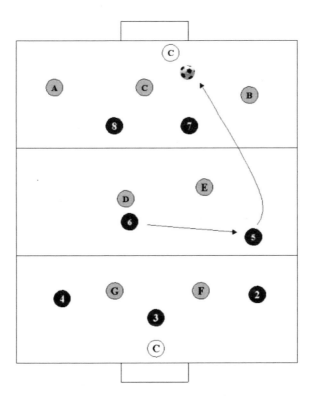

Diagram 78

1.   Here is an example of a player not pressurizing and a
     goal resulting from it. (6) passes to (5) who is not immedi-
     ately pressured by (E) and has time to play the ball into
     the hands of the coach, keeper or designated target
     player.

CHAPTER SEVEN

TEAM SHAPE AND MOVEMENT IN AN 8 v 8

TEAM MOVEMENT USING SIMPLE ONE WORD COMMANDS

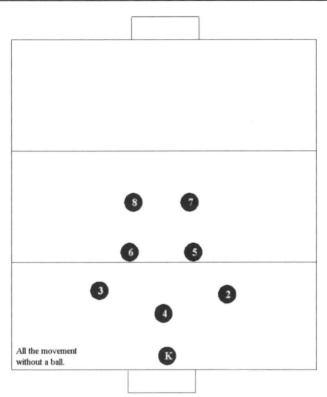

All the movement without a ball.

Diagram 79

1.   Three units of players provide a collective obstacle for the opposition to get through. By staying close together it is very difficult for the opposition to play through you because the spaces between the players are small. Force teams to go wide away from the goal.

2.   Defensive set up where the ball is in a central position with the players tight together (**compact**) both length and width wise (short and tight). It must be difficult for the opposition to play through.

3.   Set the players up in a shape and ask them to move around the field together maintaining the same spacing between each other. On command (sit) they sit down where they are positioned. This gives you a chance to check that they have kept their shape. Have words to move them again depending on where you want them to go. Words can be **UP** (up to 5 yards forward), **OUT** (a sprint, see if they can go at the same quick pace together, keeping the shape) **HOLD** (holding their position), **DROP** (retreating back towards their own goal), **SLIDE** (moving to the side). Between each word say **SIT** and check positions again.

UP

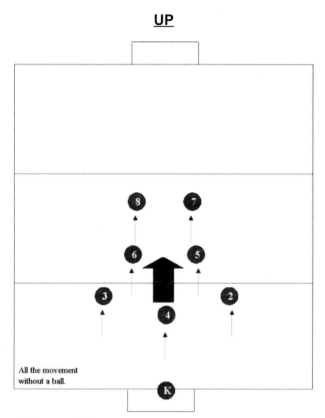

All the movement
without a ball.

Diagram 80

Game situation

1.   They have the ball and pass it back towards their own goal, for example.

2.   Here the players move up the field on the **UP** call, only up to five yards in distance, edging out, waiting to see if we win the ball then they can apply the **OUT** call.

OUT

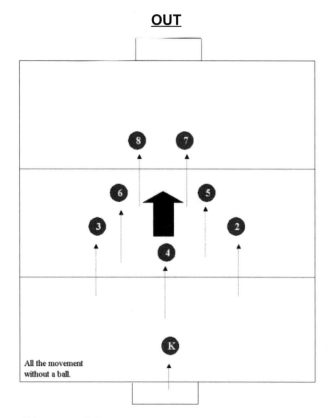

All the movement
without a ball.

Diagram 81

1.   The team **sprints out** together on the **OUT** call until you
say sit or stop. They then stop moving and sit down and
you assess their spacing between players and between
the three units. As they get good at this, speed up the
commands until they are moving around the field quickly
and efficiently with correct spacing. Eventually you can
say the different words and have them stand still rather
than sit on the **stop** command so you can move them
around the field at a faster pace working the transitions.

HOLD

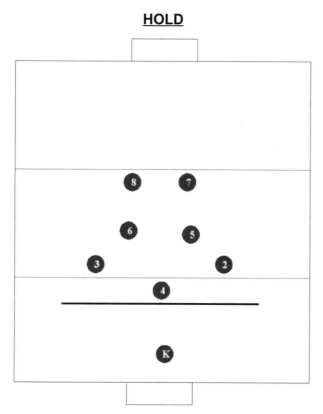

Diagram 82

Game situation

1.   There is pressure on the ball and the opponents can't pass the ball forward.

2.   Players **HOLD** the line and do not recover back. In a game situation the opponent's attackers may run forward and be allowed to run into an offside position because the ball has been stopped from forward motion by good pressurizing.

3.   The main point here is that the ball cannot be passed forward.

DROP

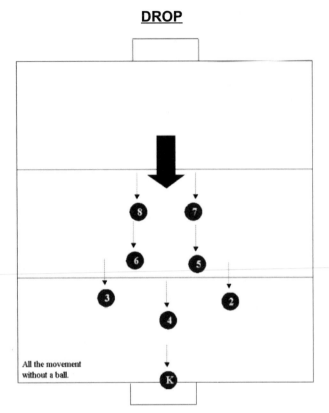

All the movement
without a ball.

Diagram 83

Game Situation

1.   Here the team drops back together recovering to the goal.
      Again, ther is more than one situation in which this hap-
      pens but it could be when the opponents have the ball
      and are moving forward and there is no pressure on the
      ball so the player on it can pass it forward and maybe in
      behind our back players. To avoid this we drop back as a
      team behind the ball.

SLIDE

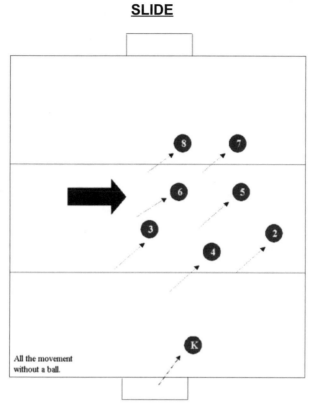

All the movement without a ball.

Diagram 84

2.   Moving across the field. In the game the ball may have been passed wide in the opponent's possession and we move across the field as a team to close down all the spaces around the ball to try to win it back.

DEFENSIVE TEAM SHAPE IN AN 8 v 8

DEFENSIVE SET UP WITH THE BALL IN A WIDE AREA

GETTING IT WRONG

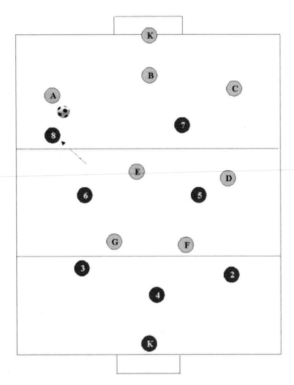

Diagram 85

1.   Here the first player pressurizes but the rest of the team stay wide and long and so don't support (8). It is unlikely that (8) can gain possession of the ball without the co-operative help of the rest of the team.

2.   (B), (C), (D), (E), (F) and (G) are all free to have the ball passed to them.

3.   Players must close up both length and width wise (short and tight as opposed to wide and long) to close spaces down around the ball and reduce the number of options for the opponents.

GETTING IT RIGHT

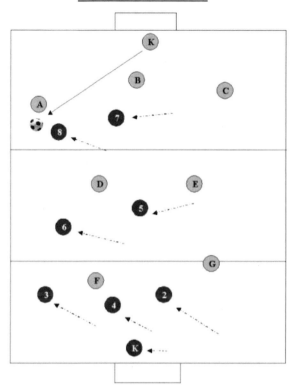

Diagram 86

1. As the ball travels, so does the team. The closest player must pressurize the player on the ball immediately with teammates in support positions. Pressing very quickly will force the opponent on the ball to make a quick decision, often forcing him to give the ball away, so the pressing player doesn't always have to actually win the ball.

2. Maintaining the shape of the team but closing down spaces around the ball, still keeping the team compact. As soon as we win the ball back we spread out as quickly as possible while keeping an eye on the player on the ball, not turning our backs to the ball (maintaining aware-ness).

WHEN THE KEEPER IS FORCED TO KICK THE BALL LONG

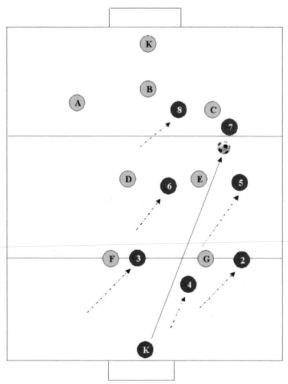

Diagram 87

1.   Decide beforehand where the keeper will kick the ball. A right footer probably will kick it to the right side. In training establish how far in distance this generally is. Position the players towards the area where the ball is going to finish so they have a better chance to gain the second ball possession. While the ideal is to play from the back there will be times when the keeper must kick it long because there are no other options on. For example, when the other team plays high pressure to stop us from playing from the back.

2.   Players must move into the area the ball is being played to as the ball travels so it is not too obvious what is happening. Occasionally the keeper can switch sides in regard to where the ball is delivered so it is less predictable.

3.   Player (8) can anticipat the flick on by (7) by making a run behind the defenders but staying onside. If (C) wins the header then the players behind the ball are in good positions to pick up the second ball.

CHAPTER EIGHT

FUNCTIONAL WORK THROUGHOUT THE UNITS

HOW TO BUILD A FUNCTIONAL SESSION

A)   Coach only one set / team of players at a time.

B)   Work with all the players on that team but work primarily with those players in the specific areas you are trying to affect. On a percentage scale consider 75% of the time with the specific players and 25% of the time with the supporting players on the same team.

C)   Stick to the same theme.

D)   Try to isolate the area of the field and the players who function within that area. For example, the area to work in with central defenders would be centrally around the edge of the penalty area up to the half way line. For wide midfielders it would be on the wings of the field.

E)   Use start positions to determine how the session begins. Servers can be used to start the session and also double up as targets to play to.

F)   Develop your theme using the key coaching points and check that you have covered them in the session.

G)   List the key points in the order you perceive them in the process of building the session.

H)   Work with the individual then the pair or unit, building up the number of players you work with at any one time.

I)   Use the functional practice to work with a small number of players in key areas of the field. A functional practice is more specific than a small – sided game, phase play or 11 v 11 and it isolates the players being coached.

J)   Once the defending principles have been established, at each stage of the practice you can make the situation competitive by counting the number of goals each team scores. The attacking team must score a goal and the defending team must score a goal by passing the ball to one of the servers without it being intercepted by an opponent.

K)   By making it competitive each team has a target to achieve.

TYPICAL EXAMPLE OF A FUNCTIONAL SET UP EXPLAINED

FUNCTION: CENTER - BACKS DEFENDING

OFFSIDE FROM THE 25 YARD LINE

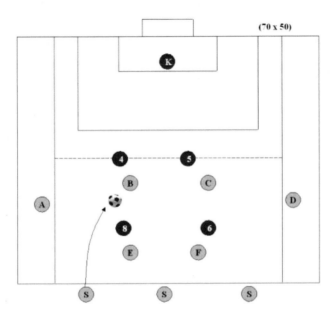

Diagram 88

1. Start Position – Have a server play the ball in to a designated player. The coach can be the server if he wants to dictate where the ball needs to go at the start, though it is better to stay out of the action and just coach the session. We are working with isolated areas on the field and certain players on a small scale.

2. Here we are coaching the two center – backs so most of the action must revolve around their defending skills. The session has been isolated to primarily coach the two players in question in the area on the field they work in. The other players' defending skills need to be coached too, but to a lesser extent.

3. A rough guide would be 75% the center – backs, 25% the

midfielders and the keeper. If the session was on defending in central midfield it would be 75% the midfielders and 25% the center – backs and keeper.

FUNCTION: CENTER - BACKS DEFENDING

OFFSIDE FROM THE 25 YARD LINE

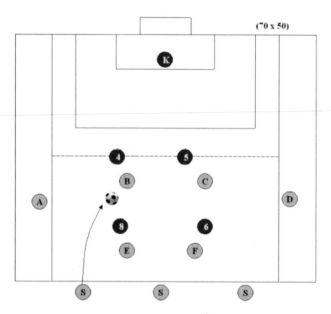

(¬0 x 50)

Diagram 89

1.   Area can be smaller to start to help defenders gain success.

2.   SP1- Server passes into (B) or (C), (4) and (5) pressure to stop them from turning.

3.   **Key Coaching Points** –
   a) Pressure on the ball.
   b) Support by the 2nd center – back (angle / distance / communication).
   c) Marking and covering (when to mark players, when to cover space).

d) Defending from crosses.
e) Get compact at every chance available (use the 25 yard line as a measure).

4.   Don't use the wide players initially.

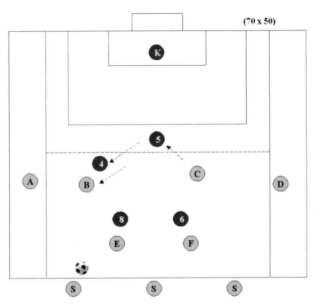

Diagram 90

1.   (B) goes wide, (4) stays tight. (5) adjusts across but with depth to cover the ball over the top in behind defender (4).

2.   At the same time, (5) takes a position to compensate for (C)'s position to prevent him from getting an unmarked run into the space behind.

3.   It is vitally important now for center – backs to communicate with each other.

4.   Introduce communication from the keeper. This is important as the keeper can see the whole field in front and can help the CB's with their positioning with regard to the strikers and blindside runs by the attacking midfielders.

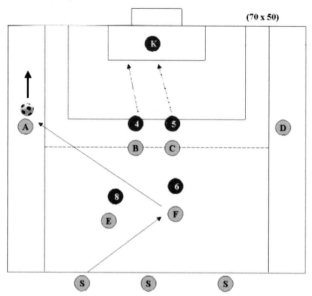

Diagram 91

1. SP2 – The center – backs now are starting closer to goal defending the edge of the penalty area. Servers can play into the attacking team's strikers or midfield players.

2. CB's must be aware of how far to track the strikers' runs back to the ball, going only so far then passing on to mid-fielders. They must be aware of the space that is left behind them if they follow too far.

3. CB's must try to avoid dropping back into the penalty area. "Hold the line" is a good call from the keeper so they don't drop back into the keeper's territory and don't allow strikers in. Introduce the wide players getting cross-es into the box for CB's to deal with. If the ball gets beyond the CB's in wide areas then they have to drop back into the box to defend the crosses. Position so they see the man they are marking and the ball.

FUNCTION: WIDE DEFENDERS (FULLBACKS) DEFENDING

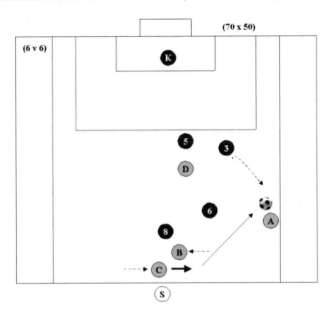

Diagram 92

1. Working with wide defender (3), who moves as the ball moves.

2. Begin each play with the midfield attacking players (B) and (C) making a crossover move. If defenders win the ball, they pass it to the server and the play restarts.

3. Decreasing the width of the area helps the defenders get early success as there is less room for the attackers to work in. To progress, open up the field when they have had enough success to gain confidence. This is a bigger test.

4. The attacking team is encouraged to get the ball wide and work with the wide attackers to get crosses in. This ensures we are concentrating primarily on the defending capabilities of the wide defenders.

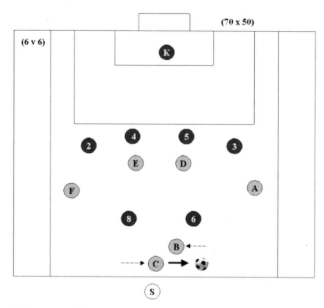

Diagram 93

1. Ball moves. Attacking team are encouraged to get the ball wide and work with the wide attackers to get crosses in. This ensures we are concentrating primarily on the defending capabilities of the wide defenders.

2. Decreasing the width of the area helps the defenders get early success as there is less room for the attackers to work in. To progress, open up the field when they have had enough success to gain confidence. This is now a bigger test.

3. Begin each play with the midfield attacking players (E) and (F) making a crossover move. If defenders win the ball they pass it to the server and the play restarts.

4. Start position 1: (E) and (F) crossover and pass the ball to a wide attacker, (A) or (D). Wide defenders (2) and (3) must then deal with a 1 v 1 situation.

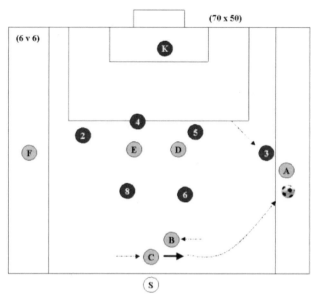

Diagram 94

1. SP 2: Move wide attackers closer to the wide defenders so they receive the ball with their backs to them. Defender works to stop them from turning and try to win the ball or at least force them to pass back.

2. This session tests the wide defenders to see if (2) and (3) can: get close enough to win the ball in a 1 v 1, stop the forward pass, stop the delivery of the cross, make play predictable by forcing the attacker to the support, recover quickly when beaten.

3. While concentrating on the wide defenders, check the positions of the other players in relation to them.

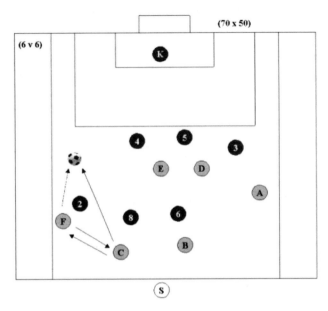

Diagram 95

1.   SP 3: (A) gets in behind (2).The ball is with (A) who plays a 1-2 with (E) (after an initial crossover move). (2) is close to (A) to begin so there is space behind to pass into.

2.   Working on (2)'s recovery run to try to stop the cross by a) (2) tackling (A), b) getting into the line of the cross to intercept, c) working back towards goal because he can't get close enough to affect the cross.

3.   Beyond the work with (2), look at the positioning of the other players when the cross gets into the box.

4.   As soon as the move is over, set it up again to test the defensive qualities of the wide defenders as they are the focus in this session.

FUNCTION: CENTRAL MIDFIELDERS DEFENDING

OFFSIDE FROM THE 25 YARD LINE

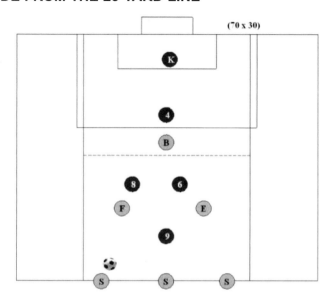

Diagram 96

1.   Three servers play the ball in from different angles.

2.   Start position 1 - passes into midfield.
SP2 - passes into striker.
SP3 - passes from wide angles to midfield or strikers.

3.   Coaching Points
a) Pressure (stopping players from turning).
b) Stopping forward passes (if player gets turned).
c) Making play predictable (forcing into the support).
d) Defensive Support (angle / distance / communication).
e) Recovery lines and distances (if the ball gets beyond the midfield).

4.   If the defenders win the ball it goes to a server and we start again.

FUNCTION: WIDE MIDFIELDERS DEFENDING

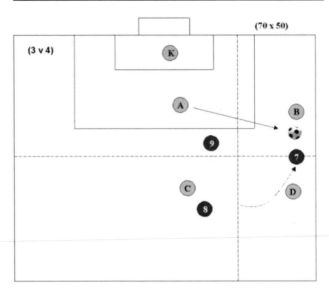

Diagram 97

1.   Working primarily with the wide midfielders (here it is 7) and how to defend in their area. If they win the ball they try to score on goal.

2.   Cone the wide area to isolate it so the wide midfielder knows the main area to work in.

   a) SP1 – Center back (A) passes to Wide defender (B), (7) pressures showing inside if possible towards the support of (8) and (9).
   b) SP2 – Center back passes to central midfielder (C), (7) must recover back to help (8).
   c) SP3 - Center back passes to the wide midfielder (D)
   d) SP4 - Center back passes anywhere and (7) adjusts accordingly.

3.   This session is particularly good if you have a small number of players at a particular session.

4.   You can make it competitive by rewarding the defending
        players for winning the ball with the chance to score a
        goal in the opponent's goal. Again you may work on the 5
        pass principle if you desire, in which they have to score a
        goal within 5 passes.

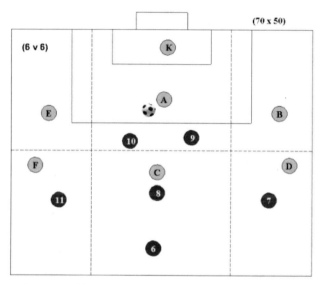

Diagram 98

1.   Develop by bringing in players to work both sides. Here
        we are working with (7) and (11).

2.   <u>Coaching points</u>:
        a) Pressing and making play predictable
        b) Support
        c) Recovering
        d) Tracking runs
        e) Doubling up

3.   Keep the main focus on the wide defenders, the other
        players in the team act as secondary support.

FUNCTION: STRIKERSDEFENDING IN THE ATTACKING THIRD IN A 2 v 3

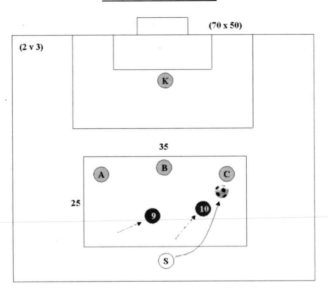

Diagram 99

1.   2 v 3 against to get strikers used to defending. The back three must work the ball over the twenty yard line to score. If the strikers win it they get a **free run at goal** to score as a reward and also to reinforce the importance of winning the ball here.

2.   Either the coach (C) initiates the play or have the keeper pass the ball to a defender.

3.   Strikers must work as a unit to try to regain possession in the Attacking third and get a quick strike on goal. This is particularly important to train strikers to learn how to defend as they are the first line of defense for the team. This can be an overlooked part of defending.

4.   The players need to realize that the closer to the goal you win the ball, the sooner you will be able to score. So practicing defending from the front is an important part of your training.

FUNCTION: STRIKERS DEFENDING IN THE ATTACKING THIRD IN A 3 v 4

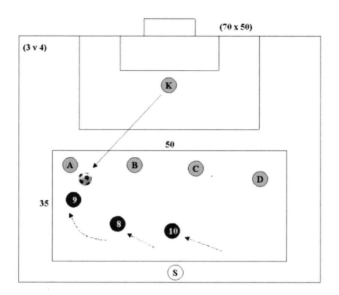

Diagram 100

1. Three defending strikers against an attacking back four. As in the previous diagram, the strikers are working on regaining possession in the attacking third.

2. The area has been increased to accommodate more players.

3. In the example above (9) forces (A) inside towards team-mates (8) and (10).

4. (8) and (10) must position close to the ball to help (9) to fill the spaces close to the ball.

5. This may tempt (A) to try to make a difficult pass to (D) who is free and if this goes wrong, the defenders are in a perfect position to intercept the pass and score.

6. This part of defending (from the front) can be over looked by coaches and players. Strikers need to be educated to

realize they have a great responsibility to help the team by defending from the front.

FUNCTION: STRIKERS DEFENDING IN THE ATTACKING THIRD IN A 3 v 3

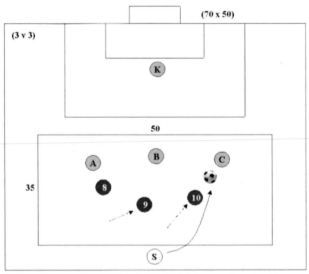

Diagram 101

1.   Here we have a 3 v 3 so the attackers should have a better chance to win back the ball and attack the goal.

2.   (10) should try to force (C) inside towards (9) and (8) for the attackers to have a better chance to win the ball.

3.   The server (or keeper) can vary where the ball is played so that each attacking player has the chance to be the first pressuring player.

4.   If it is (9) on (B) then that player has to decide which player is in the best position to support, and thus force the ball in that direction.

CONCLUSION AND DISCUSSION

We have covered the key points in defending in a logical way using defending situations from 1 v 1's through to small sided games up to 8 v 8's, 8 v 8 simplified team movements, and functional plays to show how to defend effectively.

These practices are particularly important because in many cases different numbers of players are available for training sessions. One week you may have a small number at practice, another week you may have 16 players. This book should cover most scenarios.

The practices in this book use techniques that would be applicable to 11 v 11 game situations as the same principles apply on the big stage. To study further the defending practices for phase plays and 11 v 11, see the 2nd book of this series.

By breaking defending down to key points the idea is to isolate each point and deal with it on it's own merits and then link it with other key points as they happen in the game. One can see that pressure and support go hand in hand, this is one of the most common links that occurs in the game. Recovering and tracking runs are interlinked as players need to get back behind the ball as soon as they can which involves getting back and marking space and marking players. Regaining possession is linked with advancing up the field when the opportunity presents itself. But they are all ultimately linked together and the full complement of key points of defending working together is how the team has to engage to be able to defend successfully.

Small sided games are a smaller mirrored image of the 11 v 11 game using three units of players. They are also the format used for matches at the younger age groups, so the practices in this book are applicable to all age groups.

Functional practices isolate a part of the field where certain players will play and are particularly useful to use if you have a small number of players to work with. Isolating the players and the area of the field they work in can make the session much simpler to both explain and execute for the coach and the players. All units of players are covered in this.

I hope this book has provided a basis for you to work from in the art of defending. It is particularly important for beginning the process of learning individual defending techniques and building from there.

The companion book, which covers phase plays and 11 v 11 defending, will add to the knowledge you have gained here and help you cover all aspects of defending.

Also Available from Reedswain

#185 **Conditioning for Soccer**
by Raymond Verheijen
$19.95

#188 **300 Innovative Soccer Drills**
by Roger Wilkinson and Mick Critchell
$14.95

#290 **Practice Plans for Effective Training**
by Ken Sherry
$14.95

#787 **Attacking Schemes and Training Exercises**
by Eugenio Fascetti and Romedio Scaia
$14.95

#788 **Zone Play**
by Angelo Pereni and Michele di Cesare
$14.95

#792 **120 Competitive Games and Exercises**
by Nicola Pica
$14.95

#793 **Coaching the 5-3-2**
by Eugenio Fascetti and Romedio Scaia
$14.95

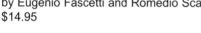

www.reedswain.com or 800-331-5191

Also Available from Reedswain